WWII GERMAN POWs IN MICHIGAN

PLANNED REEDUCATION VS. FAIR TREATMENT

Ethan Reardon

MISSION POINT PRESS

ISBN 978-1-950659-32-6

ACKNOWLEDGEMENTS

I wish to thank my thesis committee, Dr. Jay Martin, Dr. Catherine Tobin and Ms. Caity Burnell, for all of their help on this project. They provided me with valuable advice and insight into locations of information and getting funds to travel. I would like to also thank the people at the National Archives in Washington, D.C., the Frankenmuth Historical Association, the Clarke Historical Library at Central Michigan University, the Michigan State Archives, and the Lakeshore Museum Center for giving me access their archives. I would also like to thank my father James Reardon who passed away while writing this paper for all of the encouragement and time he took helping me finish this project. Without his support I would never had made it this far.

ABSTRACT

PLANNED REEDUCATION VS. FAIR TREATMENT: EFFECTS ON GERMAN PRISONERS OF WAR DURING WORLD WAR II

The story of German Prisoners of War (POW) is an often-overlooked part of the history of World War II in Michigan. German prisoners of war were kept in over thirty-two camps across both the Upper and Lower Peninsula for use as labor both in agriculture and factories. These men would see America in person instead of through German propaganda. Many POWs would form lasting friendships with American citizens that they worked beside.

With the labor program ongoing, the United States government decided that the opportunity to affect the views of the POWs was too great to simply pass over. This was done in an attempt to shift the common soldier's ideology away from National Socialism but was limited by time and staff. This thesis will examine the camps, the reeducation program, the labor program in Michigan, and their effects on the German POWs. This paper will argue that the reeducation program had a lesser impact upon POWs than the interactions with the American civilians in the labor program.

The reeducation program was hampered by poor decisions on content and was put together too late into the war to have much of an effect. The labor program allowed POWs to interact with American civilians and exposed them to American values.

TABLE OF CONTENTS

LIST OF FIGURES

CHAPTER I

INTRODUCTION

During the Second World War, the United States of America became a temporary home for over 300,000 Prisoners of War (POWs). These men came from the Axis nations: Germany, Japan, and Italy. While most were prisoners from the German army, not all were German. There were also Austrians, Poles, Hungarians, Yugoslavs, and Russians.[1] The POWs were held in camps across the United States. Rather than let the POWs sit in the camps for the rest of the war, the United States government would send the POWs to work in factories and farms across North America, where the POWs would meet ordinary Americans. To the POWs it was a view into American culture and society. For the Americans, the program let them meet the "enemy" face to face. The State of Michigan held thirty-two such camps. But this is not all that the United States government did with the POWs.

With the POWs safely tucked away in the camps, the United States government saw this as an opportunity to wean the POWs from National Socialism. The goal was to give the POWs a better idea of the values of American democracy and culture in the hope to avoid another war.[2] The purpose of this thesis is to examine both the reeducation program and the labor program in the state of Michigan and determine which was more successful in making an impression on the German POWs. I found that the labor program allowed the POWs to gain a broader understanding of the United States and its citizens than the reeducation program.

---

1. Arnold Krammer, *Nazi Prisoner of War in America* (Scarborough House/ Publishers, 1996), 149.
2. Mission and Organization of the Prisoner of War Special Projects Division, no date given; Records of the Provost Marshall General, Record Group 389, Box: 1629, National Archives at College Park, College Park, MD. 1.

Chapter I will discuss past works on this subject, their writers' views, and then discuss what I am contributing to the historiography. Chapter II covers what happened to the POWs before and after they arrived in the United States and what life was like in the camps. Chapter III covers the reeducation program from its founding to its effects on POWs after the war. Chapter IV covers the labor program and its effects on both the POWs and the American citizens that interacted with them. The conclusion reflects upon what was learned.

The internment of Japanese-Americans is well known and documented, but the story of the German POWs in the American homeland has been largely ignored. The reason might be that the internment of Japanese-Americans was a major injustice that directly impacted the freedom of American citizens while the detainment of enemy forces is regarded as simply a matter of war. One of the first books on the subject is Arnold Krammer's *Nazi Prisoners of War in America* (1979).[3] His book covered the capture of the POWs, their living arrangements, work on farms and other industries, the reeducation program, their escapes, their interactions with civilians, and their eventual repatriation. On the subject of reeducation, Krammer never gave a real opinion. He laid out the information that he has, both positive and negative, and left the reader to decide whether or not the reeducation program was effective. Krammer's work encouraged others to look deeper.

Ron Robin's *The Barbed-Wire College: Reeducating German POWs in the United States During World War II* (1995)[4] is another major work on POWs focusing more on the reeducation program. His work delved into the reeducation program that was operated by the "Idea Factory" under the Special Project Division

3. Ibid.
4. Ron Robin, *The Barbed-Wire College: Reeducating German POWS in the United States During World War II*, (New Jersey: Princeton University Press, 1995).

2

of the Office of the Provost Marshall General. However, other organizations had implemented educational programs earlier with the Provost Marshal General's blessing. The real focus of the Idea Factory was forming a special course to train POWs for work as government officials in Germany after the war. Robin claimed that the program was not very successful in its goals because of active opposition by committed Nazis in the camps and that the Idea Factory was largely made up of academics who did not understand the rank and file POW. The material produced by the Idea Factory was, in Robin's words, "highly intellectual and abstract."[5] Consequently, many of the rank-and-file POWs were not interested in nor impacted by the material.

On the opposite side of the reeducation argument is Judith Gansberg. In *Stalag: USA* (1977)[6] Gansberg focused heavily on the actions of the Special Project Division and its reeducation program. Her book was much more supportive of the program than Robin's. Using surveys that were taken by the United States government after the war at camps in New York, Nebraska, and other states, Gansberg discussed how successful the program was in convincing German POWs that National Socialism was wrong and the American way of life was better. She argued that this program contributed to the ending of the Nazi party in Germany after the war. She believed that the Special Project Division's soft approach was the safest method to reeducate the POWs because it avoided using force and overt persuasion.[7] Her argument was that even if a few POWs were turned toward democracy as a system of government then the program was a success.[8]

Other books on this topic are more focused on individual states. Robert

---

5. Ibid, 10.
6. Judith Gansberg, *Stalag: U.S.A* (New York: Thomas Y. Crowell Company, 1977)
7. Ibid, 162.
8. Ibid, 181.

Billinger's *Hitler's Soldiers in the Sunshine State* (2000)[9] focuses on the POWs held in Florida, only lightly touching on the subject of reeducation. Other books written by POWs after the war reflect upon their experiences in the United States. Detailing his time as a POW, Ernst Floeter wrote the book *I'll See You Again, Lady Liberty* (2014),[10] in which he described his experiences living in several camps across the United States.

Some historians chose to write articles or short papers instead of full books. One is *Stalag Nebraska: Labor and Education Programs in Nebraska's World War II Prisoner of War Camps* (2014) by Cole Kruger.[11] Kruger argued that it was a mixture of both the interactions of the POWs, the American civilians, and the reeducation program that led to lasting friendships between POWs and farmers.[12] His position on the reeducation program was that it was successful, and that the labor program allowed many POWs to interact with American citizens.

Regarding Michigan's involvement in the reeducation program, there is Philip Proud's history thesis written in 1949.[13] Proud took part in the reeducation program as an aid at the Fort Custer POW camp in Michigan and wrote his thesis largely based upon his personal experiences. His work gives a unique view into the reeducation program. Proud took the position that the classes provided to the

---

9. Robert Billinger, *Hitler's Soldiers in the Sunshine State*, (Florida: University Press of Florida, 2000).

10. Breen Lynne and Floeter Ernst, *I'll See You Again, Lady Liberty: The True Story of a German Prisoner of War in America* (WingSpan Press, 2014).

11. Cole Kruger, "Stalag Nebraska: Labor and Education Programs in Nebraska's World War II Prisoner of War Camps," (Master's Thesis, University of Nebraska, 2014).

12. Ibid, 18.

13. Philip Proud, "A Study of the Reeducation of German Prisoners of War at Fort Custer, Michigan, 1945-1946," (Master's Thesis, University of Michigan, 1949).

POWs by the reeducation program were a success. However, he believed the labor program impeded the reeducation program. Proud argued the camp commanders valued the labor program more and sidelined the reeducation program as a result.[14]

William Lowe from Eastern Michigan University did his Master's thesis in 1995 on the POW labor program in Michigan.[15] Because the records of the POW camps in Michigan are difficult to access in the National Archives, Lowe traveled across the state of Michigan to libraries and archives to piece together the story of the labor program from local newspaper articles. Lowe did not discuss the reeducation program; instead, he focused on examining all 32 Michigan camps to do an overview of the labor program. Lowe's work focused on telling the story of German POWs in Michigan.

A more recent view of German POWs in Michigan is a journal article "The Befriended Enemy: German Prisoners of War in Michigan" by Kevin Hall.[16] His article focused on the effects of the interactions of POWs and civilians in the state of Michigan. The article used letters written between the POWs and the farmers after the war, as well as archived accounts by local families. Some POWs sent only a few letters while others sent dozens, keeping in contact long after the war. Using this, he showed how both sides formed long-lasting friendships that endured for years after. His article briefly touches on the subject of the reeducation program, but it is not his main focus.

My reason for researching this topic is that I did not know there were

---

14. Ibid, 24.
15. William Lowe, "Working for Eighty Cents a Day: German Prisoners of War in Michigan, 1943-1946," (Master thesis, Eastern Michigan University, 1995)
16. Kevin Hall, "The Befriended Enemy: German Prisoners of War in Michigan", *Michigan Historical Review,* Vol. 41, No. 1 (Spring 2015): 57-79. Accessed: 08-10-2017, http://www.jstor.org/stable/10.5342/mich-histrevi.41.1.0057

POWs in my home state of Michigan during World War II. I discovered the subject from the State Museum in Lansing, from the single display on the topic in the World War II section. The subject got my attention, and I started looking in archives and museums for more information on the POWs that were here in Michigan. After reading a number of letters sent between the German POWs, the farmers, and their families after the war from the Frankenmuth Historical Museum, in Michigan, I noticed how friendly the POWs and the farmers became after working together. Many stayed in contact for years after the war ended. One good example is a POW named Karl J., who kept in contact with a farmer in Frankenmuth, Michigan, Otto Herzog, well into the 1950s.[17] This became a reoccurring theme among much of what I accessed.

I examined the impact of this friendship on how POWs viewed America by using a mix of letters, government documents, newspapers, and secondary sources. Many of my primary documents come from libraries, museums, and archives across the state of Michigan or from the National Archives. Most of the information on the reeducation program came from the National Archives. My research in Michigan, both in the State Archives and local archives, did not uncover much information on the reeducation program, but I did find a large amount of information on the topic of the labor program, and the interactions between the POWs and the American citizens. Quite a few POWs kept in touch with the owners of the farms where they worked. The National Archives did not keep a large amount of information on the individual camps, but I did find materials on both the reeducation program and the labor program created by the United States Government. This paper covers the evidence that I was able to access and collect from across the state and in the National archives.

---

17   . Karl J. Letters to Otto H., Frankenmuth Historical Association.

I had a difficult time collecting information while researching this topic. Most of the documents from the National Archives on the individual camps in Michigan were only lists of the number of hours the POWs worked in a month for each camp. The Archives of Michigan

Locations of POW Camps in Michigan

1 – Allegan	9 – Coloma	17 – Grant	25 – Pori
2 – Alma	10 – Croswell	18 – Grosse Ile	26 – Raco
3 – Au Train	11 – Dundee	19 – Hart	27 – Romulus
4 – Barryton	12 – Evelyn	20 – Hartford	28 – Shelby
5 – Bay City	13 – Fort Custer	21 – Lake Odessa	29 – Sidnaw
6 – Benton Harbor	14 – Fort Wayne	22 – Mattawan	30 – Sodus
7 – Blissfield	15 – Freeland	23 – Mt. Pleasant	31 – Sparta
8 – Caro	16 – Fremont	24 – Owosso	32 – Waterloo

Figure 1: Locations of POW Camps in Michigan. From Kevin Halls "The Befriended Enemy: German Prisoners of War in Michigan."[18]

had only one folder on the topic. The contents were primarily forms for hiring

18. Hall, *The Befriended Enemy,* 59

POWs and other documents relating to the labor emergency that Michigan farmers experienced during the war.

Kevin Hall recommended that I contact museums across the State of Michigan that had collections of POW letters that he had used in his article.[19] In total, 32 camps were set up across Michigan over the course of three years. Around 5,000 to 8,000 German POWs passed through the state.[20]

With the evidence that I found, I came to the conclusion that the local interactions between the POWs by the farmers and their families accomplished more than the reeducation program. This shows through in the letters and personal experiences of the POWs and local farmers. Many of the books and articles on this subject only focus on the effects of the reeducation program and barely touch on how the labor program affected the POWs. Some touch on how a combination of both led to better relations, but never really dedicate any real time discussing this. This subject is important because the labor program was just as important, if not more important, than the reeducation program in giving the POWs a better appreciation for the culture and people of the United States, as well as a better view on democracy. Too much emphasis has been put on the reeducation program, and not enough on how the fair treatment of the prisoners in the face-to-face interactions with local Americans affected German POWs.

19. Discussion with Kevin Hall, March 2016.
20. Lauran Hahn, "Germans in the Orchards: Post-World War II Letters from Ex-POW Agricultural Workers to a Midwestern Farmer". *The Journal of the Midwest Modern Language Association*, Vol. 33/34, no. 3/4. (Autumn, 2000 – Winter, 2001) pp. 170. http://www.jstor.org/stable/1315350

CHAPTER II

THE CONVENTION, THE CAPTURE, THE CAMPS

The Second World War started with Hitler's invasion of Poland in September 1939. With the surrender of the Polish government and military forces by the end of September 1939, both the German and Russian armies took thousands of prisoners. By August 1942 Great Britain was having trouble handling all of the German POWs who were taken from the last three years of fighting. At this point in the war, Great Britain held around 23,000 German and 250,000 Italian prisoners.[21] Caring for the POWs put a strain on resources already taxed by the German submarine campaign on British trade routes. With the United States now in the war, the British hoped that the United States would accept some of the POWs already held and POWs taken in the future. However, the United States came into the war with its own ideas on how to fight and did not want to enter into any agreement that would restrict its ability to act independently.[22] An agreement on the POW problem was not dealt with until the success in North Africa and the large-scale transport of POWs to mainland North America, would begin in the middle of 1943.[23] These POWs would be the first of over 300,000 German POWs to arrive in the United States over the course of the war.

The Geneva Convention

At the start of World War II the United States did not have complete freedom to treat the POWs as they pleased. In 1932 the United States signed the

---

21. George Lewis and John Mewha, *History of Prisoners of War Utilization by the United States Army 1776-1945* (University Press of the Pacific, 2002), 83.
22. Krammer, *Nazi Prisoners of War,* 1.
23 Lewis and Mewha, *History of Prisoners of War,* 90.

1929 Convention relative to the Treatment of Prisoners of War.[24] This convention was the only treaty that both the United States and Germany had signed concerning the treatment of POWs before the Second World War. The Convention was an extension on The Hague Conventions of 1899 and 1907 to cover some of the problems with POWs that had appeared in the First World War.[25] At the start of the war the United States State Department asked the Swiss Government to inform all enemy nations that the United States would comply with the 1929 Convention. All nations quickly replied that they would do the same.[26] The United States had decided early on to follow the Convention as closely as possible to keep the Axis nations from retaliating on American prisoners.[27] In Report Number 141, in September of 1943, the Office of the Provost Marshall General stated that the 1929 Convention was being "carefully followed and scrupulously observed by the United States Army."[28]

The care of the POWs fell under the control of the Prisoner of War Division of the Provost Marshall General.[29] This division was split into three branches: the Information Bureau, which controlled correspondence and was responsible for keeping records; the Operations Branch, which ran the camps and escort companies; and the Legal Branch, which dealt with all legal concerns as well as drawing up

24. "Convention relative to the Treatment of Prisoners of War. Geneva, 27 July 1929," International Committee of the Red Cross, Accessed: 04/7/2017, https://ihl-databases.icrc.org/applic/ihl/ihl.nsf/Treaty.xsp?action=openDocument&documentId=0BDEDDD046FDEBA9C-12563CD002D69B1
25. Ibid.
26. Lewis and Mewha, *History of Prisoner of War*, 75.
27. Prisoners of War, Report Number 141, September 1943; Records of the Provost Marshall General, Record Group 389, Box 2712; National Archives at College Park, College Park, MD. 1.
28. Ibid.
29. Report 141, Box 2712, 5.

any changes to the regulations concerning the POWs.[30] The Information Bureau in particular had many problems at the start of 1943, because of staffing shortages. One subsequent issue was that names were not being properly sent to the Swiss, who were serving as a diplomatic intermediary, and as a result mail was sent to the wrong camps and even the wrong country.[31]

With the start of the war, the United States had to reactivate the Office of the Provost Marshall General responsible for not only dealing with POWs but also law enforcement in the army. The position had been used on and off from the first Provost Marshall General that was created during the Revolutionary War. In 1924, Brigadier General S. D. Rockenbach was ordered to draft a manual outlining out the rules and regulations that the military would follow concerning POWs.[32] The position was eliminated in 1927 but the manual was updated in 1937 to incorporate the Geneva Convention of 1929. The Office of the Provost Marshall General was reactivated in 1941 under the command of Major General Allen Gullion, who set to work establishing the camps and support structure needed to hold POWs.[33] Gullion would remain the Provost Marshal General until 1944.

Capture

The first major influx of German POWs to come to the United States from the North African campaign in 1943 was composed of soldiers from General Erwin Rommel's Afrika Korps. Issues with the Americans' staff shortage became apparent immediately, when they found that they lacked enough German translators. At the start of the war, the intelligence agencies had quickly started to recruit translators, leaving few competent translators for the POW camps. This became more of a

30. Ibid, 5.
31. Report 141, Box 2712, 5.
32. Lewis and Mewha, *History of Prisoner of War,* 67.
33. Also was responsible for setting up the Military Police for the army.

problem at the camps where camp commanders had to depend on English speaking POWs to serve both as spokesmen and to give orders to POWs.[34] Another problem that the American soldiers had at the front lines was that not all of the soldiers in the Afrika Korps were German. Hitler's conquests in Europe as well as his alliances with nations like Italy meant that the Korps was composed of soldiers of different nationalities. Some prisoners captured by the Allies in Africa were from Poland, Hungary, Serbia, France, Finland, Belgium, Lithuania, Estonia, and the Ukraine. Many did not speak German.

All of these soldiers went through the same processing system to be sent from the front lines to the camps. After being stripped of military equipment, wounded POWs would be sent to receive treatment at medical centers alongside wounded American. Everyone else would undergo a basic medical examination. All POWs received unique serial numbers. These numbers followed them throughout the rest of their time in captivity. Each number was made up of three parts. The first was a number representing the theater in which they were captured. For example, 81 was assigned to POWs from North Africa. Five was the Western Defense Command and 31 was the European Theater. After that there was a letter representing the country of origin: G for German, I for Italian, and A for Austrian. The final set of numbers was an individual number for that POW.[35] For example a German captured in the European Theater might receive an ID number of 31G-78941.

Another problem that plagued the Office of the Provost Marshall was that there was very little inter-agency cooperation between the branches of the American

34. Ibid, 4.
35. Prisoner of War Circular No. 1, Regulations Governing Prisoners of War, September 24 1943; Records of the Provost Marshall General, Record Group 389, Box 2; National Archives at College Park, College Park, MD. 11-12.

armed services. Believing that the space would be better used for combat troops, the top commanders in the North African Theater refused to allow POW processing units near the front. Intelligence officers would take POWs' *Soldbuchs* (ID papers containing a soldier's military history, training, rank, etc.) and not return them. The processing officers would then have the POWs fill out basic paperwork such as personal records, fingerprints, information tag, serial number and a photograph.[36] All of this information was used to keep track of POWs as they were sent across the United States.

After spending time in the processing center, the POWs were loaded onto cargo ships that had just unloaded their cargo and were returning to the United States. Command decided it was faster and easier to just load the POWs onto the empty ships than it was to organize more ships to bring the POWs over to North America. The convoy system also helped protect the ships from roaming German U-boats, and no ships carrying POWs were sunk on the crossing. These cargo ships were unloaded in one of two ports, either Norfolk, Virginia, or Camp Shanks, New York.[37] One POW described the first time he saw New York City: "What a sight it was passing Manhattan. The skyscrapers were all lit up. There were cars, people, life! It was like Utopia, coming from dark Europe. The thought came to me that many hard-core Nazis would have a hard time believing this sight as they had fixed in their minds a destroyed New York."[38] Once ashore the POWs were given clean clothes and another medical check as well as any shots they needed before being allowed onto train cars for the next step in their journey. Banned personal belongings that POWs managed to keep were sent to one of two warehouses at Fort Meade, Maryland, where they were to be stored until the end of the war.[39]

36. Report 141, Box 2712, 6.
37. Krammer, *Nazi Prisoners of War,* 17.
38 0, *I'll See You Again,* 47.
39. Ibid, 6.

During all of this the Intelligence Division looked for any high value POWs, like officers or war criminals, that had slipped through the first screening process at the front. Unlike the British, the United States did not interrogate every POW.[40]

The train rides were largely uneventful. Many POWs were surprised to find that they were being transported in train coaches instead of boxcars as in Germany. As they traveled across the country to the camps, they were amazed by the size of the country and the lack of destruction that they had been told was inflicted on the United States by the Luftwaffe. Some believed that the routes for the trains were planned to avoid damaged areas.[41] Trains became the main way for POWs to be transported across large distances. Many of the main camps were located close to a railroad depot for this very reason.[42] This allowed the army to keep a closer eye on the POWs and decrease the chances of a POW escaping while being transferred from one transport to the next. One POW noted, "There were a couple of guards in the front and back of each car. If you had to use the bathroom, you had to raise your hand, and a guard would escort you."[43]

Life in the Camps

In 1943 the Office of the Provost Marshall General ordered the construction of camps for the first 50,000 POWs coming from the British that the United States had agreed to house. Many were converted from old Civilian Conservation Corps camps that were built during the Great Depression to provide work for the unemployed. These places were perfect for their new role. They were already built to the necessary requirements set by the Convention and located

---

40. Krammer, *Nazi Prisoners of War,* 18.
41. Ibid, 25.
42. Gansburg, *Stalag: USA,* 20.
43. Lewis Carlson, *We Were Each Other's Prisoners: An Oral History of World War II* (New York: Basic Books, 1997), 21.

in rural areas.[44] This meant that the POWs would be far away from important industrial locations and were in rural areas where the labor program could make good use of them as workers on farms. This was also convenient for the guards because these locations made it easier to prevent escape attempts. By the end of the war 155 base camps and over 500 new temporary work camps were constructed.[45]

Figure 2: German POW Camps in the United States. From GenTracer.org[46]

44. Krammer, *Nazi Prisoners of War,* 26.
45. Carlson, xx.
46. GenTracer, "POW Camps Map", GenTracer.org, accessed: June 5, 2018, https://www.gentracer.org/powcamps.html

Base camps were larger permanent locations, while work camps were only temporary. Most of these camps were in the South and Southwest to decrease costs in the winter, but other camps were built to provide labor in other areas of the country.

The Army Corps of Engineers built the camps with a set size of 350 acres and 500 feet outside of any important boundary or public area. These larger camps were designed to contain between 2,000 and 4,000 prisoners, normally divided into four compounds with four barracks of 150 men.[47] Included was a mess hall, workshop, canteen, infirmary, administrative building, and a recreation hall. The barracks were 20 feet by 100 feet on a concrete slab which was covered by tar paper or corrugated tin. There was a potbelly stove in the center for heating. The only real difference between a POW camp and an Army camp was the watchtowers and the fences.[48] Officers had their own camps that were larger and nicer than the ones for enlisted troops. There were very few Americans stationed inside the POW enclosure itself. Security was enforced through the guard towers and vehicle patrols. Normal procedure was to use the POWs military hierarchy to keep control.[49] Because of the language barrier and the lack of German translators, the POWs were allowed to choose their own camp spokesman.

Life in the camps was good for the POWs in the United States. The United States had an abundance of resources and had few problems keeping up with the standards set by the Convention. The Convention stated that "basic daily food rations shall be sufficient in quantity, quality and variety to keep prisoners of war in good health and to prevent loss of weight or the development of nutritional

---

47. Krammer, *Nazi Prisoners of War,* 28.
48. Ibid, 28.
49. Ibid, 161.

deficiencies."[50] The food that was provided was the same as was available to American GIs at their bases.[51] One POW wrote: "Here we eat more in a single day than during a whole week at home."[52]

Efforts were made to find something for the POWs to do to pass the time while imprisoned. Libraries and newspapers were supplied both by War Prisoners' Aid Committee of the International YMCA and the International Red Cross.[53] From the very beginning these activities, and the labor program implemented later, would take a lot of time out of their day. Almost as soon as they arrived, they elected a Study Leader who was in charge of organizing classes. The POWs consisted of teachers, carpenters, watchmakers, lawyers, mechanics, bank clerks, and many other occupations. There was a massive pool of potential classes available. According to Arnold Krammer, by 1943 almost every major camp had classes in English, Spanish, German literature, shorthand, commerce, chemistry, and mathematics. Some of these classes were so effective that in May of 1944 the German Reich Ministry of Education offered full high school and university credit for taking these courses in the camps. Booklets were sent to the United States, and POW professors could fill out the course and grade for a POW. Many of these were accepted at universities in Germany after the war.[54] POWs had the opportunity to find other ways to pass the time. Sports were the most popular. Soccer was the most popular sport across all the camps. Plays and music were also really popular with some groups forming full orchestras.[55] There were also craft centers, and in

---

50. International Committee of the Red Cross. "Convention relative to the treatment of Prisoners of War. Geneva, 27 July 1929, Article 26.
51. Gansburg, *Stalag: USA*, 22.
52. Ibid, 22.
53. Krammer, *Nazi Prisoners of War*, 206.
54. Ibid, 62-63.
55. Ibid, 52.

some cases the POWs would pool their money and buy film projectors to watch movies. Out of all of the programs and activities that were available, it was the education programs that were the most popular with POWs.

These camps all across the United States were home to over 400,000 prisoners of war for the next 4 years. With everything set up, both POWs and their guards waited out the rest of the war. Even early on there were groups in the United States government talking about doing more than just holding the former soldiers and sending them back home without doing anything to try to prevent National Socialism from rising again.

CHAPTER III

THE SPECIAL PROJECTS DIVISION AND

ITS REEDUCATION PROGRAM

The reeducation program developed by the Office of the Provost Marshall General spent a great deal of time in the planning stages and almost did not come to fruition. At the start of the war, the War Department was only interested in holding the POWs and not trying to bring about some great change in their ideology. Others led by Eleanor Roosevelt felt that something had to be done.[56] The reeducation program was the result of their efforts. This chapter will cover the ideals of National Socialism, the reeducation program, the camp newspaper *Der Ruf*, the classrooms, and a special school in Fort Eustis, Virginia for training POWs as government workers upon their return to occupied Germany.

National Socialism

The meaning of the word "Nazi" has changed over the years after the Second World War. It is now used more as a reference to somebody who is stubbornly restrictive about something.[57] According to Andrei Znamenski, National Socialism or Nazism is a form of egalitarianism and socialism with a strong mix of nationalism at its heart.[58] The full name of Hitler's party was the National Socialist German Workers' Party (Nationalsozialistische Deutsche Arbeiterpartei).[59] In order to better understand Nazi Germany, the State Department commissioned a special report on National Socialism in late 1942 to early 1943. The report outlined the

---

56. Robin, *The Barbed-Wire College,* 27.
57. Andrei Znamenski, ""National Socialists" to "Nazi": History, Politics, and the English Language," *The Independent Review,* Vol. 19, No. 4 (Spring 2015): 540, accessed January 20, 2018, http://www.jstor.org/stable/24563068
58. Ibid, 545.
59. Ibid, 539.

basic ideological concepts of the Nazi party: the *Volk* (People), racial supremacy, the leadership principle, rule by an elite class or single party, the totalitarian state, *Lebensraum*, and the use of military force as an instrument of policy.[60]

One of the core concepts of Nazi ideology was the idea of the *Volk,* or the precedence of community interests over the interests of the individual. This translates to the individual only being worth what they can contribute to the to the greater whole.[61] Along with this was the idea of Racial supremacy, in the belief that German people were superior to all others.[62] To the Nazis, the German people were simply better than other ethnic groups. To govern, the Nazis had a very simple dictatorship. This leadership principle can also be called the *Fuhrer* principle, the leader is to embody and give expression to the aspirations and wishes of the people.[63] Underneath the *Fuhrer* was the elite class or the party. In Nazi Germany's case, it was the Nazi party which served as the instrument of the *Fuhrer* to enact Hitler's orders. The state of Germany was all-powerful and strove to attain control over the lives of its subjects.[64] In order for the German people to flourish, new lands and resources would need to be opened up for the people to grow into. This was called *Lebensraum. Lebensraum* translates as "living-space" in German.[65] War however, was seen as the instrument which would allow the German people to achieve both the land and resources that they needed.[66]

---

60. Raymond E. Murphy, Francis B. Stevens, Howard Trivers and Joseph M. Roland, *National Socialism: Basic Principles, Their Application By The Nazi Party's Foreign Organization, And The Use Of Germans Abroad For Nazi Aims* (Washington, United States Government Printing Office, 1943), 5.
61. Ibid, 5.
62. Ibid, 8.
63. Ibid, 11.
64. Ibid, 14-15.
65. Ibid, 17.
66. Ibid, 19.

It is interesting to note however, that the numbers changed for how many POWs were considered Nazis. The War Department in February 1943 only had two categories: "anti-Nazi" and "others."[67] By July, 1943 it was "Nazi" and "others." By 1944 the War Department realized that this did not help identify the estimated 8 to 12 percent of hard core Nazis and the other 40 percent that were Nazi sympathizers.[68] The War Department had to change what was considered a Nazi so many times that, when a Colonel Russel Sweet of the Intelligence Division was confronted about the problem, he claimed that Nazis could be re-classified any time the War Department wanted for the good of the order of the camps.[69]

With solid understanding of the ideology that the Provost Marshall Generals Office had to combat, in a memo from acting Adjutant General Robert Dunlop to Commanding officers dated November 9, 1944, explained what the program aimed to accomplish:

> The purpose of the program is to create and foster spontaneous responses on the part of German prisoners of war towards activities and contacts which will encourage an attitude of respect on their part for American institutions, traditions, and ways of life and thought. Thereby they may be brought to realize the industrial might and indomitable spirit of the American people.[70]

In order to accomplish this, the POWs would be exposed to "facts" and through this "German prisoners of war might understand and believe historical and ethical truth as generally conceived by Western civilization...."[71] This was done to undermine Nazi ideology without using obvious propaganda methods.

---

67. Krammer, *Nazi Prisoners of War*, 184.
68. Ibid, 184.
69. Ibid, 184-185.
70. Memo from Acting Adjutant General Robert Dunlop to Commanding officers, November 9, 1944; Records of the Provost Marshall General, Record Group 389, Box: 2706, National Archives at College Park, College Park, MD. 1.
71. Krammer, *Nazi Prisoners of War*, 197.

Planning Stages

The United States was not the first nation to implement a POW reeducation program. The Russians had a program that started in October of 1941 spearheaded by Walter Ulbricht, a former Reichstag deputy and member of the German Communist Party (KPD).[72] Ulbricht fled from Germany after the Nazis took power and ended up in Moscow where he and other communist exiles formed the "Nationalkomitee 'Freies Deutschland'" or the NKFD.[73] However, Ulbricht found little support from POWs in the camps early in the war due to outdated ideas that came more from the 1920s, rather than the 1930s to which many rank and file soldiers were accustomed.[74]

In March of 1943, Assistant Secretary of War John McCloy began to talk about coming up with a plan through which "prisoners might be exposed to the facts of American history, the workings of democracy, and the contribution to America made by peoples of all national origins."[75] However the plan that was developed at that time was opposed by leaders in the American Armed Forces. The rush to set up the camps and poor officers assigned to them hampered attempts to set up a reeducation program at that time.[76] The POW camps were a popular dumping ground for American officers who were retired or found unsatisfactory for combat.[77] Many could barely speak German and had no experience dealing with POWs. With all of the staffing problems, there was not a lot of interest in

---

72 Arthur Smith, *The War for the German Mind: Re-educating Hitler's Soldiers* (Oxford: Berghahn Books, 1996), 4.
73. Ibid, 4.
74. Ibid, 8.
75. Ibid, 10.
76. Robin, *The Barbed-Wire College,* 22.
77. Gansberg, *Stalag: USA,* 42-43.

adding more in the form of a reeducation program. One of the biggest opponents of a reeducation program was the current Provost Marshal General, Allen Gullion.[78] In a letter to his commanding officer, the Chief of Staff of Army Service Forces, Gullion discussed his fear that the Germans would try the same thing with United States POWs held in Germany.[79] Gullion believed that the prisoners were people who were smart enough to sense that they were being manipulated. They already had their "philosophical frameworks" in place and were not worth the effort to influence.[80] Due to the perceived problems, the War Department shelved the plan for the next few months as the first POWs arrived on mass from the African front. The logistical challenges of the POWs arrival along with building and organizing the camps took priority over ideas to change the incoming prisoners' world views. The subject of reeducation was not touched by the military for yet another year.[81]

By 1944 the situation involving the war and POWs had changed. The call to reeducate the POWs was becoming stronger from both citizens and politicians concerned about the future of Germany and America's role in building it. By 1943, some members of the public started to realize the opportunity that the United States had with the POWs. One of the earliest references to the reeducation of POWs was in a letter to the editor of the *New York Times* on April 17, 1943, from H. Landsberg:

> In the meantime there exist the possibility of experimenting to some extent with various methods that might help in the re-education process. Already a considerable number of enemy prisoners are in our hands, and in their camps introduction of certain educational methods may help in testing procedures to be followed later on in occupied territory.[82]

78. Robin, *The Barbed-Wire College,* 22.
79. Ibid, 22.
80. Ibid, 22.
81. Gensburg, *Stalag: USA,* 60.
82. H. Landsberg, "Education Against Fascism, "*New York Times,* April 12, 1943, final edition, in New York Times Archives (accessed June 5, 2017).

Landsberg was not the only one to notice that the United States Government was missing a golden opportunity. Other letters to the *New York Times* followed, but by late 1944 all of the letters, editorials, committees and groups promoting a POW reeducation program the War Department were met with silence. Finally, the Harvard branch of the American Defense Organization sent a resolution to the Secretary of War Henry Stimson on a reeducation plan.[83] Stimson responded by rejecting the proposal and stated that the War Department was doing everything that it could and that such a program would be met with suspicion and resistance by the POWs.[84]

However, the War Department's apparent public rejection of a reeducation program belied what was actually happening. In reality, by late 1944 the War Department was already implementing a reeducation plan. This happened after Eleanor Roosevelt got involved and talked to the President, who talked to the Secretaries of War and State, who in turn talked to the Provost Marshal General.[85] Mrs. Roosevelt had been approached by the *New York Herald Tribune* about the problems in the camps with the hardcore Nazis.[86] Planning started in early 1944 on a reeducation program. With the increased pressure from the public and other political officials, the War Department began to see the value of reeducation and started to look for ways to start a reeducation program that would not cause the Germans to retaliate on American GIs. The answer was found in Article 17 of the Convention, which stated: "Belligerents shall encourage as much as possible

83. "Stimson Rejects Plan to Teach Nazi War Prisoners Democracy," *New York Times,* November 30,1944, final edition, in New York Times Archive (accessed June 5, 2017).
84. Ibid.
85. Krammer, *Nazi Prisoners of War,* 195.
86. Ibid, 195.

the organization of intellectual and sporting pursuits by the prisoners of war."[87]

This article of the convention was the foundation of the reeducation program and allowed the Office of the Provost Marshall General to look at the older plan that had been rejected in 1943. On top of this new enthusiasm, in May 1944 Major General Archer Lerch was promoted to Provost Marshall General.[88] He was more open to the idea of POW reeducation and he quickly started working with the Secretary of State Edward Stettinius and Secretary of War Henry Stimson to design an appropriate program.[89]

The man assigned to build and administer the program was Lieutenant Colonel Edward Davison. Davison was a poet and professor of English literature at the universities of Colorado and Miami before the war, and afterward he would go on to become the dean of Hunters College's Schools of General Studies.[90] He was assigned to direct the new Special Project Division (SPD) branch of the Office of the Provost Marshall. Davison was an interesting choice. He was born in Britain, had no experience with German culture, could neither read nor speak German, and was a heavy critic of capitalism. Davison's problem with capitalism is well shown in his poem "Decline and Fall" (1937):

> England Farewell! And you, America, you
> Who might have saved the spark that was divine,
> Go Down! Morgan and ford and Hearst and all
> The Dollar Gods you trusted, they are through,
> And what you signed upon the dotted line
> Has now become the Writing on the Wall.[91]

---

87. International Committee of the Red Cross. "Convention relative to the treatment of Prisoners of War. Geneva, 27 July 1929, Article 17.
88. Gansburg, *Stalag: USA,* 62.
89. Ibid, 62.
90. Ibid, 62-63.
91. Robin, *The Barbed-Wire College,* 44.

Another major player in the reeducation program was Major Maxwell McKnight who would serve as the administrative director allowing Davison to work on the education program.[92] By late 1944 the final plan was put together and an outline was sent out to all camp commanders explaining the program.

To help the reeducation program, the Office of the Provost Marshal started to crack down on the Nazis in the camps. Earlier the camp officials were willing to allow POWs to elect their own camp leader to serve as a liaison with camp staff. Because most of the POWs could not speak English and most of the camps staff could not speak German, many of the speakers were either Nazis or leaning in that direction. Much of the daily running of the camps was left to the Non-Commissioned Officers (NCOs) of the POWs. The Convention did not force the NCOs into the labor program, and this gave them plenty of time to reassert military discipline in the camps.[93] Many camp commanders early on allowed the Nazis to control the camps because the Nazis kept things quiet and under control without causing major problems.[94] The commanders were more focused on keeping upwards of hundreds of trained soldiers quiet and under control than dealing with political ideology. One POW described it best: "I thought we had gotten away from the Nazis, but I erred. In every camp, these brutes had their commandos and kangaroo courts. They would make POWs with different political beliefs from theirs get out of bed at night and then condemn them to death, either by hanging or clubbing."[95] Most of these efforts failed as camp officers used the programs designed to separate Nazis from non-Nazis as a place to put troublemakers. The

92. Ibid, 46.
93. Ibid, 32.
94. Krammer, *Nazi Prisoners of War,* 181.
95. Lynne and Ernst, *I'll See You Again,* 50.

separation of Nazis and non-Nazis ended in the middle of 1945 with the end of the fighting in Europe.[96]

Another problem in the camps was the lack of well-informed camp personnel. As camp personnel and POWs interacted, it was inevitable that politics would be discussed between them. Many Nazis in the camps were well informed on the tenants of National Socialist ideology. Most American guards were not knowledgeable enough about democratic ideology to counter the POWs arguments. In order to help counter what was seen as the lies spread by Hitler, the Office of the Provost Marshal published a 13-page booklet called "Facts vs Fantasy" which listed the more common arguments made by POWs and suppling what it called "The Facts" on each one.[97] The United States Government hoped that this would help to further undermine the control of the Nazi ideology in the camps.

With the fresh attempt to separate the Nazi element from non-Nazis in the camps, the United States Government went to work to put its reeducation plan in action. But how would the Special Projects Division accomplish this task? They could not force the POWs into classes in America. Any blatant attempt to spread anti-Nazi propaganda would only make the POWs resist and may have caused POWs working in the labor program to find ways to retaliate. This would not only hurt any further attempts to reeducate the POWs, but also put future relations between the United States and Germany in doubt. Thus, it was decided by the government in 1944 to label the program top secret to prevent any of this from happening.[98]

---

96. Krammer, *Nazi Prisoners of War,* 186.
97. War Department, *Facts Vs Fantasy* (Washington: United States Government Printing Office, 1944).
98. Special to The New York Times, June 14, 1945; Records of the Provost Marshall General, Record Group 389, Box: 1597, National Archives at College Park, College Park, MD. 1.

In order to reach the POWs without them becoming aware of the reeducation program, the members of the Special Projects Division chose to control what newspapers, films, books, and other sources of media that the POWs had available to them. This was allowed by Article 17 of the Convention where the detaining power held the right to encourage intellectual pursuits.[99] The Special Projects Division created a list of books, newspapers and movies that the POWs were allowed to view. At the same time, the Special Projects Division began to remove books, newspapers, and movies that put the United States in a negative light and seemed to uphold the ideals of the National Socialist party.

One example of "good books" was a 24-title collection called *Bucher-reihe Neue Welt* (New World Bookshelf).[100] Books that had been banned by the Nazi government, like Thomas Mann's *Achtung Europa* (Attention Europe), and *Der Zauberberg* (The Magic Mountain), Carl Zuckmayer's *Der Hauptmann von Koepenick* (The Captain from Koepenick); and Heinrich Heine's *Meisterwerke in Vers und Prosa* (Masterworks in Verse and Prose) were part of the New World Bookshelf.[101] This was followed by American books translated into German from authors like Joseph Conrad, Ernest Hemingway, and William Saroyan.[102] These books were chosen based on how far they stayed away from Nazi ideology.

In order to implement the reeducation program, service commands in the camps were given Assistant Executive Officers who would be responsible for the program.[103] Their task was to implement the programs, monitor the effects, and report back to headquarters. To recruit these officers, Davison held five conferences

---

99. International Committee of the Red Cross. "Convention relative to the treatment of Prisoners of War. Geneva, 27 July 1929, Article 17.
100. Krammer, *Nazi Prisoners of War,* 207.
101. Ibid, 207.
102. Ibid, 207.
103. War Department, 2.

of 100 men each. Men were selected based on qualifications listed in their records and had three days to decide whether or not they were competent to work in the reeducation program.[104] About 40% were screened out during the conferences. Many of them had lied about being able to speak German and others left when they found out that there was little opportunity for promotion. Most of them did not believe it would work and that it was a waste of time. In the end, 262 officers and 111 enlisted men were picked and trained to serve at the POW camps and other service command headquarters as overseers of the programs.[105] With the plan and personnel in place, Colonel Davison set out to build the team that would monitor, censure, and edit all the movies, books and newspapers that would be permitted in POW camps across the nation.

Der Ruf

The newspaper *Der Ruf* was originally planned by the United States Army to reach the more common POWs in the camps that were not interested in attending the classes or going to watch all of the movies. Newspapers were popular with POWs who were very interested in finding out more about not only their homeland and news of the war but also sports and other activities to pass the time. The first issue of *Der Ruf* had 11,000 copies printed and sold 10,000, according to a report by the Provost Marshal General's Office.[106] The last issue of *Der Ruf* in April, 1946 had 73,000 copies sent out.[107]

To spearhead the team responsible for the creation of the newspaper, Davison set out to find someone who knew German language and culture to

---

104. Krammer, *Nazi Prisoners of War,* 199.
105. Ibid, 199-200.
106. Captain James Wilson, "Distribution and Sales *"Der Ruf""*", May 15 1945; Records of the Provost Marshall General, Record Group 389, Box: 1597, National Archives at College Park, College Park, MD. 1.
107. Krammer, *Nazi Prisoners of War,* 204.

serve as the head of the staff. As many Americans with the required skills were already recruited by other branches of the military, this proved a problem. Davison eventually chose an exiled German novelist and former associate editor of the liberal newspaper *Das Berliner Tagblatt*, Captain Walter Schoenstedt.[108] At the time, Schoenstedt was working with the army's Morale Division's "Know your Enemy" pamphlets for the armed forces.[109] It fell to Schoenstedt to oversee the writing of the paper, as well as finding anti-Nazis with the right qualifications to serve as the editorial staff. Schoenstedt handpicked all members of the POW newspaper staff to work on *Der Ruf*. He filled these spaces with people like him: alienated German intellectuals, disillusioned Communists, writers, and journalists. [110] In total 85 POWs would be selected for the newspaper staff and split up into 6 groups. One group would focus on translation of POW newspapers into English and reeducation material into German. Another group would review POW newspapers, while another would review plays, music, and books to decide if they fit with the goals of the program. There was one group for films. Another group handled the publication of *Der Ruf*, while an additional command group coordinated the work of all.[111]

As the first home for the program, the Special Projects Division decided to set up the POW staff for the newspaper in a camp at Van Etten, New York. This was later changed to Fort Philip Kearny, Rhode Island.[112] Fort Kearny was originally an artillery post established to protect the area around Narragansett Bay in the early 1900s. The guns were removed at the beginning of the war as other naval defenses in the area were seen as more important. The Special Projects

---

108. Robin, *The Barbed-Wire College*, 46.
109. Ibid, 46.
110. Ibid, 60.
111. Gansburg, *Stalag: USA*, 70-71.
112. Ibid, 67.

Division took advantage of this and took control as a POW camp. The total group of 85 anti-Nazis came to be called "The Idea Factory" at Fort Kearny.[113] Since all of the POWs at Fort Kearny had been specially screened and verified before being accepted into the program, they were permitted more freedom than other camps.[114] Many of the POWs were committed anti-Nazis, all were former Wehrmacht officers, and most were educated men.[115] The paper was published bi-monthly and available in all camps.[116] With the infrastructure set up, the staff started working on *Der Ruf* in January 1945 with the first issue released in March of 1945.[117] *Der Ruf* was made available for $0.05 at the camps' canteens.[118] The money generated was used to fund more Special Projects Division programs, like buying books and supplying films.

The paper almost immediately received mixed views from not only the POWs in the camps but with American officials who worked with either the Office of the Provost Marshal or the War Department. One memorandum made by a welfare officer responsible for an unknown number of camps stated that, while it sold well in one camp, in others it was openly ridiculed.[119] One criticism that one officer noted across many of the camps was that of the items printed under the

---

113. Krammer, *Nazi Prisoners of War,* 200.
114. Gansberg, *Stalag: USA,* 68.
115. Krammer, *Nazi Prisoners of War,* 201.
116. National German Prisoner of War Magazine *"Der Ruf"*, February 8, 1945; Records of the Provost Marshall General, Record Group 389, Box 2706; National Archives at College Park, College Park, MD. 1
117. Smith, *The War for the German Mind,* 82-83.
118. Printing of German Language Newspaper, January 24, 1945; Records of the Provost Marshall General, Record Group 389, Box 1597; National Archives at College Park, College Park, MD.
119. Statements made by Welfare Officers Relative to *"Der Ruf"* and the Value of American Films, undated; Records of the Provost Marshall General, Record Group 389, Box 1597; National Archives at College Park, College Park, MD. 1

heading "Voice of the Camps" were the work of one individual.[120] An unknown army officer working with POWs overseas wrote his thoughts on reading the two papers released in April of 1945. His comments made it all the way up to Provost Marshal General Lerch:

> If the publication is intended to have some influence in dispelling Nazi ideology, then it falls very wide of the mark. Editorially, the issue confines itself to exhortation to the P.W.'s to face the future with courage and determination. To re-educate the P.W.'s politically, a radically different approach would obviously be necessary.[121]

The main issue was that the paper was too academic for the rank and file POWs. The head of the Special Project Division, Colonel Davison, shared this concern about the first issue of the paper. A few days before the paper was available to the POWs, Davison spoke with Schoenstedt, claiming he felt that "the newspaper's text was dense to the point of being incomprehensible."[122]

This problem plagued the paper up until the program was ended. This is best shown by a German university professor in a letter he sent to the Provost Marshal Office in September 1945. In it he writes "Numbers 9 and 11 of this periodical *"Der Ruf"* smack too much of educational journals and have too many articles. The average war prisoner has neither the inward calm nor the inclination to read them. As we have already said the prisoner wants to hear a great deal about Germany."[123] This assessment was a long-term problem with the paper that was never really solved. *Der Ruf* was written for a level of education that many POWs

120. Ibid, 1

121. Comments on the 1th of April 1945 Issue of *"Der Ruf"*, Records of the Provost Marshall General, Record Group 389, Box 1597; National Archives at College Park, College Park, MD. 1.

122. Smith, *The War for the German Mind,* 76.

123. Expression of opinion concerning the War Prisoners periodical *"Der Ruf"*, August 13, 1945; Records of the Provost Marshall General, Record Group 389, Box 1597; National Archives at College Park, College Park, MD. 2.

did not have. Many of the letters and criticisms of the paper revolved around the fact that the paper was too "high-brow" and that it would benefit from sections on sports and comics.[124] The paper ended up reading like a university paper that many of its editors and writers were used to writing and reading, rather than a mainstream paper to which the common POW was accustomed.

A good example of this is in one of the two front page articles from the first issue of *Der Ruf*. The article "The Inner Power" was one of the first articles in *Der Ruf* and showcases what many of the articles looked like.[125] "The Inner Powers" was an appeal to intellect, but was too obviously a critique of National Socialism. The article could also be taken in other ways. At the anti-Nazi Camp Devens, Massachusetts, the POWs claimed "The Inner Powers" was "hidden Nazi Propaganda" because it did not have any "aim or positive thought."[126] On the other hand, the Nazi's at Camp Aliceville, Alabama called "The Inner Powers" an anti-Nazi article because "it was diametrically opposed to the basic Nazi philosophy that the state, rather than the individual spirit, is all-important."[127]

Other criticisms for the paper came not only from officers informed on the program, but from the POWs themselves. In some cases, there were active attempts to keep the paper off the shelves by more hardline Nazis. At one camp in Georgia the entire stock of the paper was bought and burned by group leaders who viewed it as anti-Nazi propaganda.[128] Some camp leaders ordered other POWs to not buy the paper. The paper was sometimes destroyed by POWs and the stewards at the

124. Comments on the 15th of April 1945 Issue of *"Der Ruf"*, Records of the Provost Marshall General, Record Group 389, Box 1597; National Archives at College Park, College Park, MD. 3.
125. See Appendix 1.
126. Robin, *The Barbed-Wire College,* 76.
127. Ibid, 76.
128. Letter from Brigadier General Bryan Assistant the Provost Marshal General, April 18, 1945; Records of the Provost Marshall General, Record Group 389, Box 1597; National Archives at College Park, College Park, MD.

canteens were threatened with harm if they continued to put it on the shelves.[129] A few POWs called it propaganda almost immediately.[130]

However not every initial reaction was negative. In a Texas main camp and some of its branch camps, the paper was well received. The camp spokesman, Alfens Reffgen, stated that, *"Der Ruf* seems to have the type of material that will appeal to all prisoners. It is highly objective and creates no suspicion of Propaganda."[131] The POWs at Camp Ruston, Louisiana, also liked the paper with a report stating:

> At this installation, German prisoner response to the initial issue of "Der Ruf" was most enthusiastic. Since there is no POW camp newspaper published here, the need for a sort of paper like "Der Ruf" is great. Increased circulation with the next issue has been requested by the prisoners in all compounds and branch camps. [132]

In a telephone call between a Colonel Rogers and Major Taylor on the subject of *Der Ruf* in an area controlled by the 8th Service Command, Taylor claimed that the copies he received were nowhere near enough for the interest that the POWs were showing in it.[133] Many POWs who liked the paper or were on the

129. Field Report, *"Der Ruf"*, March 28, 1945; Records of the Provost Marshall General, Record Group 389, Box 1597; National Archives at College Park, College Park, MD. 1.
130. Spot Check on Sale of *"Der Ruf"*. March 10, 1945; Records of the Provost Marshall General, Record Group 389, Box 1597; National Archives at College Park, College Park, MD. 1.
131. *"Der Ruf"*, March 13, 1945; Records of the Provost Marshall General, Record Group 389, Box 1597; National Archives at College Park, College Park, MD. 1.
132. Reactions to "Der Ruf"; Records of the Provost Marshall General, Record Group 389, Box 1597; National Archives at College Park, College Park, MD. 4.
133. Transcription of telephone conversations between Col. Roger, and Major Taylor, 8th S.C., March 12, 1945; Records of the Provost Marshall

fence requested that the paper have more on music, literature, and art to draw more attention.[134]

Over time editors and writers made only small attempts to correct this issue, and the papers content changed little. The paper further isolated itself by almost never having news from Germany. By the time that the paper was introduced into the POW camps, the war was almost over and everyone knew it. Many of the POWs were thinking of home, how their families were doing, and the condition of their nation. However, *Der Ruf* was never intended to operate alone. The Intellectual Diversion Program went to rework the schools set up by the POWs.

Schools

Other than the newspaper and censuring the books and the reading material allowed in the camp stores and libraries, the Intellectual Diversion Program would also offer courses in the camps on subjects deemed appropriate.[135] Before the Intellectual Diversion Program was put into action, POWs were permitted to set up their own schools in their camps. POWs could organize classes, lectures, studies and discussion groups on any subject within reason.[136] Prisoners would then elect a director of studies to run and manage the different programs.[137] POWs who had been civilian teachers, carpenters, watchmakers, and every other occupation

General, Record Group 389, Box 1597; National Archives at College Park, College Park, MD. 1.

134. Spot Check on Sale of *"Der Ruf"*, March 1945; Records of the Provost Marshall General, Record Group 389, Box 1597; National Archives at College Park, College Park, MD. 1.

135. Intellectual Diversion Program, November 9, 1944; Records of the Provost Marshall General, Record Group 389, Box 2706; National Archives at College Park, College Park, MD. 2.

136. Prisoner of War Circular No. 46, October 13, 1944; Records of the Provost Marshall General, Record Group 389, Box 2; National Archives at College Park, College Park, MD. 1.

137. Ibid, 1.

imaginable put together classes.[138] This gave the POWs the chance to use their time in the United States productively to learn new skills or even finish their education interrupted by the war. Some of these courses were so successful that the Reich Ministry of Education offered full high school and university credit for completing them.[139]

When the Intellectual Diversion Program was in the planning stages, the organizers wanted to influence the programs already in effect in the camps. It was simply easier to use the existing schools than to start over again. The reeducation program made more classes available, but this time they were controlled by the Special Projects Division with teachers screened and monitored by the Special Projects Division. The reading of hundreds of books and films was put under the control of the staff at The Idea Factory on top of their work on *Der Ruf*. Before the reeducation program started, the POW schools got their books from the International Red Cross. Some were even provided directly by the German government.[140] After the purges and book burnings in the 1930s, many of the approved books from the German government were not going to pass the new requirements for the reeducation program. These books were removed and replaced with books approved by the staff at The Idea Factory.

The Assistant Executive Officer of each camp was responsible for establishing the reeducation program in the camps. These officers traveled to the camps to re-examine the schools that the POWs had set up. Classes that officers found did not benefit the reeducation program were removed. Classes in English, American history, geography, and civics were offered.[141] English classes were pushed hard to make the task of teaching American ideas easier. To help get more

138. Krammer, *Nazi Prisoners of War*, 62.
139. Ibid, 62-63.
140. Ibid, 206.
141. Gansberg, *Stalag: USA*, 93.

POWs in the classrooms, the Special Projects Division approached universities near local camps and asked them to provide approved classes.[142] The effectiveness of the reeducation program depended on the Assistant Executive Officers' skills and enthusiasm for the program at the individual camps. Some camps saw large changes in the programs while others saw none at all.

The war came to an end for the German POWs on May 8, 1945, with the surrender of Germany. The reeducation program was in full swing. With the war coming to a close, the War Department turned its attention to determining how to administer the new United States Zone in occupied Germany. The War Department decided to train some of the POWs in the camps to serve as administrators and policemen. They were already in the United States and could be screened far more reliably. The War Department gave approval and one school for each was put together focusing on the English language, one school for American and German history together, and one on the structure of civil and military government.[143] With the war over, the Office of the Provost Marshal decided to declassify the reeducation program by giving a press report on the program to major newspapers and use it and the new schools as public relations tools.[144]

With the secret reeducation program now out in the open, the camps were notified to screen POWs to look for suitable students for the new schools. Any Nazis were to be rejected immediately. The schools started in May 1945 and the final class ended in October of that year. A total of 1,166 POWs went through the program and received special certificates that could be used to get a position in the Military Government that was running post-war Germany. However, an issue came up almost as soon as the POWs arrived back in Germany. The Military Government

142. Ibid, 95.
143. Krammer, *Nazi Prisoners of War,* 219.
144. Smith, *The War for the German Mind,* 97.

showed little or no interest in using the POWs. The POWs were largely ignored by the occupation government that in many cases did not even know about the project.[145] The Military Government was not officially notified of the special POW camps.[146] On top of this, the POWs in the program had to be rescreened under the Military Government Law No. 8 which forbid anyone from the Nazi party from regaining a position of influence. This meant that many POWs from the programs were barred from working.[147]

With all the programs now running out in the open in 1945 there was a snag. After the war ended, the POWs were not sent back right away. It was decided by the War Department that the POWs would not be sent home to Germany like the Convention ordered. Instead, an agreement was made between the Allies in which many POWs would be sent to France and England to help rebuild the countries as forced labor.[148] Many POWs in the camps felt like they had been betrayed. They had believed that they would go straight home, not be sent into forced labor in France. This issue threatened to undo much of the good will for the United States for which the heads of the Special Projects Division had worked.[149] The Division rushed to put together a program to "educate" as many POWs they could.

In response to labor camps in France, the Idea Factory quickly put together a 6-day crash-course program for 20,000 POWs. According to the head of the Special Projects Division, the goal of the program was "To inculcate in 20,000 selected cooperative German prisoners of war such understanding and attitudes concerning democratic experience in the United States, Germany and the world, as will contribute most to the building of a more democratic, peaceful,

145. Krammer, *Nazi Prisoners of War,* 219-220.
146. Smith, *The War for the German Mind,* 160.
147. Ibid, 156.
148. Ibid, 242-243.
149. Ibid, 243

and cooperative Germany."[150] POWs were chosen from lists supplied by camp commanders of any anti-Nazis that resided there. These POWs had to then take a short questionnaire, and this would be judged by the staff at The Idea Factory and labeled 'white' for pass, 'grey' for undecided, and 'black' for Nazi.[151] Anyone who had any connection to the Nazi party was automatically disqualified. Because many associations were connected to the German government, all workers or members of those associations were part of the Nazi party even if only in name.[152] This meant that the vast majority of POWs were not allowed to participate in the program. Those allowed were then sent to Fort Eustis, Virginia, to attend classes. By the end of the program, 23,142 POWs would graduate from Fort Eustis, Virginia.[153]

The classes were fast paced and covered every subject from the American Constitution, the Bill of Rights, education, and political parties. There were movies and discussions after that.[154] Overcrowding was a massive problem. Because the War Department wanted the POWs sent back as soon as possible, the program was rushed to the point that at any time there were double the number of POWs at the fort than there was space to teach. This led to over half of the POW population at the time sitting around waiting for space to open in the classes.[155] Resources had to be shifted to provide activity for those waiting. The activities included mostly films, some English instruction, musical recordings, and sports.[156]

In the end, the War Department took a poll to find out if the opinions of the POWs had changed after participating in the Fort Eustis program. This poll contained three groups: One from the Fort Eustis who had gone through the speed

150. Smith, *The War for the German Mind*, 98.
151. Robin, *The Barbed-Wire College*, 150.
152. Ibid, 150.
153. Smith, *The War for the German Mind*, 100.
154. Ibid, 99.
155. Ibid, 100.
156. Ibid, 100.

course of reeducation, one from Camp Shanks in New York made up of 22,153 POWs from all nine service commands, and a group from Atlanta, Nebraska.[157] According to this data of the 13 questions asked, 8 reflected the impact of countering Nazi indoctrination with a 64% positive result in the favor of American democracy.[158] When looking at the questions one by one, some gave alarming answers. The group at Camp Shanks showed that 57% believed that the Jews were at least partially to blame for the war. Even the Fort Eustis group had a 10% response suggesting Jewish guilt in the war.[159] The data appeared even worse for the Camp Shanks group. On the question of the Holocaust, 38% percent believed that it was propaganda, and 32% gave no comment.[160] The report then went on to say:

> It was roughly estimated by many intelligence officers who had worked in prisoner of war camps that the political attitudes of German prisoners of war prior to the inception of the re-education program could be divided into three categories: 13% Nazi; 13% anti-Nazi; and 74% neutral. If these figures were at all reliable it appears that the re-education program was effective in changing 23% to a strong anti-Nazi force and changing 61% from a neutral to a positive appreciation of democracy, but in reducing the Nazi strength by only 3%.[161]

However, there is a problem with this data. No poll was performed before the reeducation program was started so no real comparison can be made on how much changed. The poll also did not seem to consider any other conditions affecting the POW response. What some never questioned is that some POWs may have just answered in a way that they knew the Americans wanted.

157. Poll of German Prisoner of War Opinion, Date unknown; Records of the Provost Marshall General, Record Group 389, Box 1655; National Archives at College Park, College Park, MD. 1-2.
158. Ibid, 5.
159. Ibid, 9.
160. Ibid, 15.
161. Ibid, 29.

In July of 1945 two social scientists named Donald McGranahan and Morris Janowitz did a similar poll of young Germans both in Germany and in camps in France. They argued that the quick response to questions in a democratic manner was the result of an ingrained attitude of "implicit and uncritical submission to authority."[162] The prisoners were simply very familiar with the answers that were expected, rather than a change in ideology.

In the end only 26,000 POWs were permitted in the Fort Eustis, Virginia, program. This means that only 5.4% of POWs nationwide went through the Fort Eustis program. This is a small number for any program, especially with over 300,000 POWs across the country. There is also the fact that all POWs in this program were all screened beforehand for Nazi ideals. Any POW that went through the Eustis program would have to have been screened as an anti-Nazi. POWs who were Nazi or in the middle were never permitted to enter the program. The classes in the camps across the country were smaller and more able to respond to individual issues.

Michigan and Reeducation

Most of the information on the reeducation program in Michigan comes from Fort Custer. This installation was located on the border of Kalamazoo and Calhoun Counties, and was the main base camp for Michigan's POW camps. Fort Custer was the only camp in the Lower Peninsula that operated year-round. A few in the Upper Peninsula worked year-round helping logging companies, like Camp Evelyn and Camp AuTrain in Alger County, Camp Pori and Camp Sidnaw in Houghton County, and Camp Raco in Chippewa County.[163] POWs were sent in the warmer seasons to the branch camps to work on the different labor programs

---

162. Robin, *The Barbed-Wire College,* 164.
163. John Pepin, "POW Camps in the U.P." *Marquette Mining Journal,* (January 2000): 1.

and then return to either Fort Custer or other main camps in the Great Lakes region in the winter. Many of these branch camps only lasted a few months and were never used again. This was done to shift POWs to locations that needed labor the most. This temporary nature meant that most of the camps did not keep much information relating to the reeducation program. While many of the temporary camps would have a small library, they did not keep many records because of the camps temporary nature.[164]

The national POW newspaper *Der Ruf* was not popular with the men in Michigan. Philip Proud's 1949 thesis on the reeducation program at Fort Custer argued that *Der Ruf* was seen as obnoxious by the POWs.[165] Proud himself worked on the reeducation program at Fort Custer as an aide to First Lieutenant Paul W. Schwiebert who was the Assistant Executive Officer.[166] Far more popular at Fort Custer was a paper made by POWs called *Die Bruecke* (The Bridge) that was published weekly. *Die Bruecke* was more popular because it did what *Der Ruf* did not. It had a local news and sports section that covered topics and issues more important to the common POW and was not purely an academic or intellectual paper.[167]

As for the education programs, Fort Custer had the normal run of classes, and its books and material were subject to the same monitoring as other camps. In January 1945 there were 42 classes with a total of 1,062 students enrolled. English was one of the most popular classes.[168] With the start of the program in early 1945, the school at Fort Custer slowly removed classes that did not fit into

---

164. Ibid, 2.
165. Proud, *A Study of the Reeducation,* 59.
166. Ibid, 17.
167. I could find very little on *Die Bruecke* and the sources used, then Proud did his thesis in 1949. (ibid. 62.)
168. Ibid, 68.

the reeducation philosophy and replaced them with approved classes. The POW libraries were also purged in the same manner. However, not everything went well as Proud listed a few issues with teaching POWs:

1) The Students were prisoners, as well as the teachers, occasioning very obvious limitations.
2) Ages of these students ranged from 14 to 62.
3) Educational backgrounds ranged from slightly more than nothing all the way to doctors' degrees.
4) Nationalities within the group included Germans, Austrians, Poles, Czechs, Hungarians, Slavs, a Spaniard, and an Arab who could not speak German.
5) The American personnel was limited to two.
6) Both students and teachers were subject to transfer at any time. This means constant changes in the number of classes and the curriculum. It also created a problem in certification of achievement.
7) Prisoners worked on different shifts necessitating the scheduling of classes at unusual hours.
8) Most of the teachers were voluntary.
9) Finances were limited.
10) Many American officers and enlisted men were suspicious, yet the program could not be explained at this time because of its classification as secret.[169]

The Assistant Executive Officer in the camp tried to make changes to help solve the problems that the reeducation program encountered. Signs and instructions were changed to both German and English. The camp newspaper printed some materials in English. Classes were scheduled for both morning and evening sessions. The Assistant Executive Officer made other small changes to make the curriculum simpler. [170]

Overall the effects in Michigan of the reeducation program were minimal to nonexistent. The only newspaper the Special Projects Division distributed was

---

169. Ibid, 71.
170. Ibid, 72.

too intellectual for most POWs. The education program was only for those who registered for classes. It would not reach people who did not want to spend their limited free time in the class room when there were many other things to do like sports or hobbies. Many POWs were sent to branch camps and worked for months at a time, which interrupted the learning process. On top of this, the Fort Eustis program only had about 5.4% of all POWs take part. With only 5,000-8,000 POWs in Michigan over the course of the war, the program would have touched the lives of few Michigan POWs.[171]

The English classes in the camps most likely had the largest effect on the POWs' world view. The ability to read and speak English not only allowed POWs to read new books that they may have not had access to in German, but it also gave the POWs the ability to speak to people other than Germans. This allowed the POWs more interaction with American civilians. Such classes had more of a benefit than classes in U. S. History or Geography.

Another problem with the reeducation program was the apparent lack of thought into how hard it might be to try and change a person's world view. The entire program revolved around information control and school style classes. When the reeducation program was formed, many military officers were against reeducation based on the fact that the POWs were not children and that they already had most of their views set. To change people's views requires them to be influenced by life experiences, events, connections with others, and the environment.[172] The

171. Hahn, *Germans in the Orchards,* 170.
172. Susan M. Yelich Biniecki, and Simone C. O. Conceicao, "How living or traveling to foreign locations influences adults' worldviews and impacts personal identity," *New Horizons In Adult Education & Human Resource Development 26,* no. 3 (2014): 40, accessed January 20, 2018, http://web.a.ebscohost.com.cmich.idm.oclc.org/ehost/detail/detail?vid=0&sid=67fbdbd0-eb26-44ee-ab88-789a5b00d6e1%40sessionmgr4010&bdata=JnNpdGU9ZWhvc3QtbGl2ZQ%3d%3d#AN=97162841&db=ofs

environment can impact how people perceive themselves, interact with others, and act in the world.[173] The consequence of being imprisoned in a POW camp in another country, opened new experiences for POWs to reexamine their views of the world. A deep-seated change in a person's views can only come about when the social/cultural, motivational, and cognitive dimensions of teaching and learning are integrated.[174] In other words, the POWs had to be able to put what they learned in class into practice. However, allowing the Nazis among the POWs to reinstate control and implement military discipline had the opposite effect. It was done to keep the POWs under control, but it meant that anything learned in the classrooms was known by the hardcore Nazis in the camps. One POW remembered how Nazis were in every camp and would regularly attack POWs with the "wrong views".[175] An example was the murder of Corp. Hugo Krauss and four other POWs, in Camp Hearne, Texas. On December 23, 1943, six to ten men entered his barracks and beat him to death while his barracks mates watched. He had been a very vocal anti-Nazi.[176] The labor program provided a way around this by allowing POWs to travel outside of the camps, but was underutilized by the educators.

The heads of the reeducation program seemed to ignore the fact that the POWs were in fact POWs, and that normal educational methods did not work well in the environment of the camps.[177] This fact did more to undermine the reeducation

173. Ibid., 41.
174. Karen Murphy, "Teaching as Persuasion: A New Metaphor for a New Decade," *Theory Into Practice,* Vol. 40, no. 4, (Autumn, 2001): 226, accessed January 20, 2018, http://www.jstor.org/stable/1477483
175. Breen and Floeter, *I'll See You Again,* 50.
176. Russell Porter, "Ex-Yorkville Man slain As Prisoner," *New York Times,* January 17, 1945, final edition, in New York Times Archive (accessed June 5, 2017).
177. Robins, *The Barbed-Wire College,* 183-184.

program than anything else. These POWs were not college students going to class to learn, but soldiers that had been captured by the enemy.

CHAPTER III

THE LABOR PROGRAM AND CIVILIAN INTERACTIONS

When the United States entered the war, it was not completely prepared to fight a large-scale conflict. With the military's size increasing, a civilian manpower shortage was unavoidable. The use of POWs to cover the shortages, especially in farming, freed badly needed manpower in support of the war effort. The labor program would greatly aid farmers from all corners of the United States. This would provide the POWs the chance to see America for themselves. This chapter will cover the history of POW labor in the United States, its establishment, other nations labor use, Michigan's experience, and the effect that interacting with civilians had on POWs.

History of POW Labor in the US

The United States first gained experience with using POW labor during the Revolutionary War. At the time the care of POWs was left to the local towns and states. One example of this early treatment was with a group of Scottish Highland Regulars captured in June 1776. They were given to the State of Virginia by the army. From there Virginia sent noncommissioned officers to places on the frontier and the rest of the soldiers to live with families throughout the state. The POWs were employed by locals and paid wages based on skill and ability. Richard Henry Lee stated that this allowed POWs "....to become the Citizens of America instead of its enemies."[178] The idea that giving POWs the chance to see how American ideas work proved to be successful. After the war some Hessians who fought for the British and were captured by the Americans indebted themselves to American businesses so that they would not be sent back to Europe. Others were allowed

---

178. Lewis and Mewha, *History of Prisoner of War,* 15.

to stay if they paid 80 Spanish milled dollars. Around 6,000 of these soldiers remained in the United States after the war.[179]

The American Civil War was the United States' first taste of large-scale prisoner handling.[180] Most of the POWs spent their time incarcerated in camps and were not used for labor. The only exception to this was those exchanged for other captured soldiers between both sides. It was not until the First World War that large scale planning on how to utilize POW labor took place. Due to how late in the war the United States entered, the POWs were never used in large numbers in the United States homeland, with only 5,887 being documented.[181] There were POWs used in non-combat support roles under the American Expeditionary Force (AEF), but this work remained in France.[182]

The Labor Program in World War II

The Office of the Provost Marshal decided early on to use POWs to help deal with the labor problems that would arise from the increase in size of the United States military. With the labor shortage during World War II, Washington passed the Emergency Farm Labor Act.[183] This mobilized local resources to help but also allowed the use of POWs as farm labor. Not only would using the POWs help the war effort, but it would also keep the POWs occupied. By 1942 the labor problem had not yet become critical, and the Office of the Provost Marshal spent only a little time creating a contract system where businesses could hire POWs to cover for losses in manpower.[184] The small number of POWs in the United States

179. Ibid, 20.
180. Ibid, 27.
181. Ibid, 57.
182. Ibid, 61.
183. A.B. Love and H.P. Gaston, "Michigan's Emergency Farm Labor, 1943-1947," *Extension Bulletin 288,* Michigan State College-Extension Service (December 1947), 3.
184. Ibid, 101.

at the time meant that the large-scale use of POW labor was impossible and most work was limited to military bases. From the end of 1942 to the beginning of 1943 the manpower shortage became more pronounced. More men were joining the war effort or moving to cities to work in the factories. It was at this time that the Office of the Provost Marshal started to work with the War Manpower Commission to find which areas of the United States were hit the hardest by the manpower shortages. The idea was to find which areas and industries needed help the most and transport the POWs to those areas. The main camps where located in places that allowed for easy distribution to smaller branch camps where seasonal labor could be utilized. The use of the Civilian Conservation Corps (CCC) camps allowed many smaller branch camps to be established in only a few days. This meant that POW labor could be sent anywhere in the United States. The process of hiring POWs was sent through to the Office of the Provost Marshal directly to work out each contract with the employer and collect payment. Eventually the commanders of the Service Commands were given control of negotiation and collection of POW accounts to speed up the process.[185]

The use of POWs as a stopgap for labor shortages did not please everyone. Early on it was feared by the War Department that organized labor would object to POWs putting Americans out of work. Organized labor feared that employers would be able to pay POWs a lower wage. In Minnesota in 1943, local unions involved with logging objected to the use of 600 POWs sent by the War Manpower Commission to work in Minnesota. The union president claimed that while the local unions did not have the manpower needed, manpower from other industries could work in the forests.[186] The regional director of the War Manpower Commission

---

185. Ibid, 122.
186. Lewis and Mewha, *History of Prisoner of War,* 134.

considered the union position unjustified and went forward with using POWs in logging in December 1943 without further issue.[187]

With the POWs being paid the flat rate of $0.80 a day, no matter what work was performed, American labor use in many cases was more expensive than using POWs. In 1940 the average monthly wage for a farm laborer was $28.05, which equates to an average daily pay of $0.93.[188] The War Department decided to work with the Office of the Provost Marshal to set wages that POWs would be paid to appease organized labor. Eventually it was decided that POWs would be paid the $0.80, but the employer would have to pay the local going rate for that type of work to the United States government who would then take $0.80 from that to give to the POWs.[189] The difference was used by the War Department to fund other programs and projects like the reeducation program or to cover other expenses. This $0.80 was on top of $0.10 that all POWs were given each week for items like soap, toothpaste and shaving gear. Rather than pay the POWs directly, the money was converted into camp credits that could be used to buy things in camp stores. When the war ended, the POWs could collect the difference before being sent home.[190]

The POW labor program was regarded as a great success by the War Department. The use of POW labor on military bases alone saved the United States Government $131,000,000.[191] This labor not only saved the United States Government time, it freed manpower for the frontlines. Soldiers who would have

187. Ibid, 134.
188. United States, *Historical statistics of the United States, colonial times to 1970* (Washington: U.S. Dept. of Commerce, Bureau of the Census: 1975), 163.
189. Prisoner of War Circular No. 1, 36-37.
190. Krammer, *Nazi Prisoner of War,* 84.
191. Lewis and Mewha, *History of Prisoner of War,* 263.

had to be stationed stateside to maintain and clean these facilities were sent to combat positions instead.

Type of Labor

By the end of the war, over 95 of every 100 prisoners who were physically able were put to work.[192] But it took the Office of the Provost Marshal some time to determine how to get POWs cleared to work. The Geneva Convention of 1929 states clearly in Article 27 that POWs can be used as labor by the Detaining Power:

> The Detaining Power may utilize the labor of prisoners of war who are physically fit, taking into account their age, sex, rank and physical aptitude, and with a view particularly to maintaining them in a good state of physical and mental health. Non-commissioned officers who are prisoners of war shall only be required to do supervisory work. Those not so required may ask for other suitable work which shall, so far as possible, be found for them. If officers or persons of equivalent status ask for suitable work, it shall be found for them, so far as possible, but they may in no circumstances be compelled to work.[193]

The Convention then went on to describe the work POWs could do. The safety of the soldiers was a major concern for the signing powers. Article 29 protected POWs from being employed in work for which they were physically unfit.[194] This article prevented POWs who were sick, injured, or handicapped from working. Article 32 outlawed the use of POWs in work that was dangerous.[195] Work the Convention considered dangerous included things like mining which involved explosives or places that employed heavy chemicals. However, some open pit work was allowed as long as safety equipment was provided; and some POWs were allowed to work in foundries where they shoveled sand, carried, cleaned, and

192. Krammer, *Nazi Prisoner of War,* 113.
193. Convention of 1929, Article 27.
194. Ibid, Article 29.
195. Ibid, Article 32.

ground castings; loaded and unloaded cars; and aided in ladle pouring.[196] POWs involved with this work had to have had some prior experience in these industries.

Under Article 31 of the Geneva Convention POWs were not allowed to do any work that was directly connected to operations of war. Under Article 31, POWs could not be used to manufacture and transport arms, munitions, and any goods that were headed straight for the front lines.[197] However, the Geneva Convention only set basic rules as to what could and could not be done, and the War Department used this. POWs could not make tanks, but they could work with scrap iron that could be made into tanks. POWs could even be used to pick crops and work in food processing plants canning. Whether or not that canned food went to American citizens or soldiers on the frontline was ignored. Many of the Articles were vague, and there were always exceptions to the rules. POWs would find themselves employed in a wide variety of jobs. Overall the Convention could be, and was, interpreted by both sides and worked out between them.[198]

Early on, the type of labor a POW could do was split into two classes by the Provost Marshal. Class one was work required for the administration, management and maintenance of the POW camps.[199] Class two included all other types of labor that do not fall into class one, like "out of camp" work and work on military bases.[200] POWs were allowed to work on military bases as long as the base did not have a certain level of importance. One example of such a location is at Columbus Army Service Forces Depot, in Ohio. The base held 74% of the United States government's supply of raw rubber. However, in 1945 a team of POWs was

196. Lewis and Mewha, *History of Prisoner of War,* 140.
197. Convention of 1929, Article 31.
198. Krammer, *Nazi Prisoner of War,* 80-81.
199. Regulations Governing Prisoners of War, September 24, 1943; Records of the Provost Marshall General, Record Group 389, Box 2; National Archives at College Park, College Park, MD. 34.
200. Ibid, 34.

assigned to work on some of the buildings on base. Nothing negative happened, but after this the Office of the Provost Marshal paid more attention to where POWs were permitted to work.[201]

Most of the work done by POWs was in agriculture across most of the continental United States. There were only a few strikes by POWs refusing to work, but camp commanders used a simple "No Work- No Eat" method. It was feared that if German POWs in the United States pulled off a strike, American POWs in Germany would try it and cause both sides to take more extreme measures.[202] That is not to say that POWs who refused to work starved, but they would be put on bread and water if they refused to work. POWs on bread and water for a few days quickly went back to work.

By the end of the war, POWs had worked in agriculture, logging and lumbering, food processing, meatpacking, fertilizer plants, mining and quarrying, some foundry work, and a little railroad maintenance. By June 1945 the United States Treasury had been paid $22,000,000 for work done by POWs.[203]

Michigan's Labor Experience

The first time the government used POWs in the State of Michigan as part of the labor program was on October 2, 1943, in Benton Harbor, Michigan.[204] Three hundred and seventy-four German POWs and 170 guards arrived in the city to be used as labor.[205] They were called in to work at the agricultural processing plants around the city as well as Welch's Grape Juice plants in Mattawan and Lawton.[206]

---

201. Employment of POW's at Industrial Installations, January 25, 1945; Records of the Provost Marshall General, Record Group 389, Box 2704; National Archives at College Park, College Park, MD. 1.
202. Ibid, 108.
203. Krammer, *Nazi Prisoners of War,* 107.
204. Lowe, *Working for Eighty Cents a Day,* 9.
205. Ibid, 9.
206. Ibid, 9.

The group worked in the area until a lack of labor in Tuscola County forced the POWs to be moved there on October 18, 1943.[207] The use of POWs in Michigan increased with the success of the POWs in Benton Harbor, and an increase in the need for labor led to more temporary camps all across the state by the Office of the Provost Marshal. In order to hold larger numbers of the POWs needed for labor, Fort Custer, Michigan, was refurbished as a full time POW camp. Fort Custer, however, was too far away from some of the places that needed the labor. Branch camps were established all across the state to house POWs for anywhere from a few weeks to a few months. The idea was to place POWs near areas that needed the extra labor and then send them back to Fort Custer for the non-productive colder months. However, because of the unique shape of Michigan's Upper Peninsula, the camps in the U.P. were designed differently.

Camps in the Upper Peninsula were designed to house POWs over longer periods of time than the camps in the Lower Peninsula. This was due to the POWs being used in the logging industry year-round. Only five POW camps were established in the Upper Peninsula: Camp Evelyn and Camp AuTrain in Alger County; Camp Pori near Mass City and Camp Sidnaw in Houghton County; and Camp Raco in Chippewa County.[208] In early 1943 POWs were banned from logging work because the Judge Advocate General of the Army decided that logging constituted dangerous work under the Geneva Convention.[209] This changed when an investigation by the government into the use of POWs cutting and harvesting pulp wood was preformed and showed that POWs could be used to safely perform this work with a four-day training program put in place. The War Department approved the use of POWs in this manner, and by the end of 1943, POW camps

207. Ibid,12.
208. Pepin, *POW Camps in the U.P*, 1.
209. Lewis and Mewha, *History of Prisoner of War*, 132.

were established in remote logging camps.[210] Heavy logging remained forbidden.

Life for these POWs was different from POWs in the Lower Peninsula. While it was common for those in the Upper Peninsula, most of the POWs in the Lower Peninsula did not work in the snow. Another problem was being shot at by hunters. Guards tied strips of red cloth around POWs' arms so that they would be easier to identify in the woods. Guards also encouraged POWs to sing songs loudly to scare away deer and prevent hunters from poking around.[211] Some locals remember the POWs working in the area. One local, Glen Maki, remembered working with the POWs skidding logs. "It seemed they went out of their way to be nice to me," Maki said. "I think I reminded them of their kid brother they had back home."[212] Some POWs became close enough to Americans that they met that when his wife gave birth, the POWs asked about her condition and that of the child.[213] Some POWs threw candy to local kids either on the trips to and from the work sites or in the woods.[214]

Most POWs in Michigan, however, found themselves working on local farms in the Lower Peninsula. Michigan farmers normally used out-of-state workers, but the draft and rationing of fuel and rubber made it impossible to transport the men who normally worked on the harvest. This made the use of POWs much more economical for farmers. Locations for branch camps at old CCC camps or at fairgrounds were readily available, with a total of 32 being established.[215] There on the local farms, POWs and citizens of the United States came face to face.

---

210. Ibid, 132.
211. Pepin, *POW Camps in the U.P.,* 3.
212. Ibid, 4.
213. Ibid, 5.
214. Ibid, 5.
215. Hall, *The Befriended Enemy,* 59.

Now, outside of the camps, POWs would get to see for themselves the country and lifestyle of the people living in Michigan. In turn American families would get to come face to face with the captured members of the German armed forces.

The farmers of Michigan were happy to have any help they could get. Their livelihood depended on the crops being harvested on time. Some farmers treated the POWs like any other worker who would have worked on their land. One grandson of a Frankenmuth farmer remembered the POWs that came to work on his Uncle's farm and how they were treated and behaved:

> Julius asked for a group of prisoners. About thirty came with an American guard who carried a gun, drove the truck and had charge of the group. They came in a large truck, more like a cattle truck. They parked along Lang road next to the beet field and went to work with Grandpa Zehnder and Julius.
>
> The war prisoners were furnished with food by the government, mostly army rations, peanut butter and jelly sandwiches. But our german Frankenmuth people, did not forget their Bible verse. Mathew, 10 v 10 A workman is worthy of his meat. So, Grandma Zehnder and Hildeg and made a big juicy beef roast and made hot beef sandwiches with homemade bake oven bread, pickles etc. hot coffee and milk. Hildeg and called me to help serve the lunch on the big hay rack at noon, while Grandma took care of the kids.
>
> Grandpa and Julius talked german to the guys and they were a happy group of young men. A certain percent was deducted from the beet check by the government for expenses.
>
> Julius asked the guard if he could treat the guys with a bottle of beer at mid-morning break. The guard said, "not when I'm looking, but I'm not looking all the time" So Julius gave them a bottle of beer in the morning and afternoon.
>
> The second day they came late. Grandpa and Julius were working in field already. When they finally came, they all jumped out of the truck and went to work immediately. About eleven o'clock the guard crawled out of the truck. Here, he got drunk the night before, in the morning the prisoners put him in the back of the truck with his gun and the prisoners drove the truck out to the farm and went to work.[216]

216. "Prisoners of World War II," Interview with Mike K. by Anita B.,

This treatment was not an isolated incident. Many farmers treated the POWs well. To the farmers, the POWs were badly needed labor.

Guards often did not enforce all the rules. One woman in the Frankenmuth area remembered the POWs working on their beet farm:

> Ma and Pa were told not to feed the prisoners. The Army would provide them with food. The prisoners arrived with one cheese sandwich. Pa got angry and our family started baking and cooking. Pa swept out the garage and set up saw horses and boards for a long table. He put a fire in the pot-belly stove and went back out into the field where Marv was pulling beets. As Marv finished a section, the prisoners would pick up the beets and toss them over on windrows. Marv kept pulling beets in another section and, when the prisoners got to the end of their section, Marv would hitch the wooden triangle onto the tractor and pull it through the section that was done to smooth out the ground for the trucks or the John Deere with the hay wagon attached. The prisoners would top the beets and throw them into piles. Pa came along with the scoop (?), picked them up and tossed them onto the vehicle. Sometimes it was so wet that the truck or wagon got stuck so that Pa brought the scoop full of beets all the way to the yard where the truck was sitting. By the third day, some of the prisoners would hop on the wooden triangle for the ride. The added weight would smooth the field better. ...
>
> Ma and Grandma got up early and started cooking and baking. The night before Pa had killed some chickens and Ma and Grandma had cleaned them. I also remember a roast of some sort (veal?, beef?, pork?) Marv remembers a whole ham. Lynn remembers huge amounts of boiled potatoes. I remember the DOUGHNUTS. Grandma baked lots of bread.
>
> The saw horse with the boards on top were set up in the garage. This little person had never seen the garage soooo clean and Ma's old picnic tablecloth (which wasn't long enough for the table) and, what had to be old, clean sheets on either end of the table (She wouldn't have used the linen, so it must have been sheets).
>
> After much activity in the kitchen, from which I was sent constantly, the P.O.W.'s started in from the field and the food began arriving in the garage. I was a little shorter than the table

and I couldn't see all the food. I was probably starting to climb up a saw horse to get a good look at this phenomenon when I was lifted up high above the table. Lord, was that pretty. I asked or announced, to no one in particular, "Don't the doughnuts look nice?" and turned to get an answer from the nice person who was holding me up so I could see, and, OH GOD, THERE'S A STRANGER HOLDING ME AND HE'S GOT TEARS RUNNING DOWN HIS CHEEKS and I turned with my arms out, ready to yell, and Ma grabbed me. "MA, I didn't do anything to him." And she said, "That's all right. He's got one at home about your age." Which didn't make me feel any better at that point, but it sure stuck with me for a long time, trying to figure it out.[217]

When her father Otto found that the POWs had not been supplied with good gloves, he went out and bought them gloves.[218] However not everyone was happy that he was treating the POWs so well. When some started to accuse him of "collaborating" with the enemy, he responded, "Anyone that works to get in my crops in November and December will be fed so that they don't drop from exhaustion from all the hard work and, in the freezing weather, will have gloves with which to do the work."[219]

This type of treatment was not unusual for farmers in other areas in Michigan. One farmer, William T. in Eau Claire, Michigan, would speak to the POWs while driving them back and forth from the army camp to his orchard.[220] He got to know the men with whom he worked. He asked about their families and their lives. Just like in Frankenmuth, William supplied POWs with meals, mostly spaghetti, chili or bowls of soup.[221] His kindness was remembered by the POWs long after the war. For a few years after the war, the POWs would keep in touch

217. Written statement by Verna van D., Lynn A., and Marv H., February 1995, Frankenmuth Historical Association. 1-2.
218. Ibid, 2.
219. Ibid, 2.
220. Hahn, *Germans in the Orchards*, 172.
221. Ibid, 173.

with William. The letters they sent are an interesting insight to life in post-war Germany. Johann F. wrote one such letter in poor English: "I also don't forget all that you have done for me or your farm all that good dinner and that much kake and all that play we made together!" Still others wrote about spending time during the noon break listening to one POW play the piano.[222]

William's actions, however, would sometimes dismay army officials. In one instance a POW fell off a ladder, and William drove him to the doctor to get stitches just like he would have for any of his other workers rather then send the POW back to the camp for treatment.[223] William also had a tradition of giving end-of-harvest gifts to workers. Normally this was a cash bonus after crop was harvested. But because the army would not allow POWs to receive cash, he gave the POWs warm socks and long underwear for the coming winter.[224]

In Muskegon, the owner of the North shore Celery Farm also treated the POWs like valued workers. He brought the POWs coffee and tobacco while they worked.[225] After the war the POWs wrote to the owner William B. (called Bill in the letters) asking about how he and his family were doing as well as asking for whatever aid he could give. One POW wrote, "I don't forget your humane and friendly treatment to all of us German boys (POW) compared to the bad time I spent in French."[226] The same POW kept in touch up to the 1980s right before Bill passed away. Another POW in the group, Hans S. agreed writing: "I think always that it was a fair time by you and I shall never forget it."[227]

---

222. Ibid, 173.
223. Ibid, 174.
224. Ibid, 174.
225. Hall, *The Befriended Enemy,* 71.
226. Horst B. Letter to William B., April 12, 1950, Lakeshore Museum Center, MI.
227. Hans S. Letter to William B., April 16, 1948, Lakeshore Museum Center, MI.

The farmers in Frankenmuth were not forgotten either. One Juergen K. wrote to the farmer he worked for in 1947 talking about life in Germany; "The time as a P.O.W. over there with you was like a paradise on earth compared to the present."[228] Others like Karl J. wrote Otto to "thank you more formally once more for your kindness" for all that they had done.[229] Karl later wrote:

> If you, Mr. Herzog, would come to Germany, as I remember you had in mind to do once, you surely would find what I have written to be true. If your plans should be realized, you are heartily welcome in my house. Thank God, the bomb damage is almost repaired so you could find a place to stay with me in spite of the hard times, we don't give up hope for better times to come, because as long as we live, we hope.[230]

A third POW echoed the sentiment, "Today I think back to that time in thankfulness. You and your family were so gracious and treated us with generosity those days we were there."[231] This same POW continued to write to Otto thanking him for sending food packages while he was still a POW in a French work camp.[232] The former POW would stay in contact for several years.

William T. from Eau Claire, Michigan, received 53 letters back from POWs who had worked on his farm in 1943.[233] Many of these letters were similar to others sent to Michigan farmers. The letters painted a dark picture of an utterly destroyed Europe. Some prisoners asked for pictures that had been taken while

---

228. Juergen K. Letter to Otto H., January 15, 1947, Frankenmuth Historical Association.
229. Karl J. Letter to Otto H., July 21, 1947, Frankenmuth Historical Association.
230. Karl J. Letter to Otto H., July 22, 1948, Frankenmuth Historical Association.
231. Gerolf S. Letter to Otto H., June 24, 1946, Frankenmuth Historical Association.
232. Ibid.
233. Hahn, *Germans in the Orchards,* 170.

working on William's farm. Their copies had been taken by the military police in the European work camps.[234] Others asked for him to send food to their families in Germany as they were still working in camps in France.[235] Werner M.'s postwar letter really shows how much the POWs cared about him:

> Our treatment was never anywhere near as nice at other places as it was with you, not anywhere in my entire time as a prisoner of war. I think of you as a son would think of his home, since you were then like a father to his children, who were helpless and alone in the world. I would like to thank you a thousand times for all the good things that you did for me. You gave me long underwear because I had nothing for the winter, and the socks also served me well during the cold months… When we sat at the table eating, I could almost believe that I was at home eating with my mother. With you there was the certainty that we were valued as human beings by you and your family.[236]

The impact of Michigan farmers on German POWs cannot be ignored. Many POWs fondly remembered the times spent with American families. There on the farm the POWs got away from the camps and the almost constant gaze of hardcore Nazis that had taken positions of power at the camps. It is unrealistic to think that every single work detail had a Nazi spy in it reporting back to the camp. When away from prying eyes, the POWs could relax and act more like people than soldiers captured by the enemy.

By the end of the war, the labor program would save many farmers crops from rotting in the field all across the country. The time and labor saved by using POWs allowed badly needed resources to be moved elsewhere. By 1945, 95.6 out of every 100 POWs who could be made to work under the Geneva Convention

---

234. Ibid, 176.
235. Ibid, 176.
236. Ibid, 176.

were doing so.[237] The program not only benefited the United States. Many POWs could turn in the credit that they received for working into cash that they could take back and spend in Germany. These were badly needed funds for them and their families when the POWs got back to war-torn Germany.

However, the POWs did not just take back cash. They built new friendships as well as first-hand insight into the American way of life. Working on the farms gave POWs the chance to see and interact with American democracy in action in a way that just being told about in a classroom could never accomplish. Interacting on a daily basis with American civilians allowed POWs to see American culture for themselves. The reeducation classes tried to only teach the POWs about the American way of life.

237. Krammer, *Nazi Prisoners of War,* 113.

CONCLUSION

The Second World War was a unique experience for the United States. Not only did the United States fight Germany and her allies in Europe, but also fought against Japan in the Pacific. The POWs were a problem for which the United States was hardly ready. It is amazing that the POW camps worked as well as they did. The attempts to follow the Geneva Convention as closely as possible was, by some accounts, a major reason for so many German soldiers to simply give up at the end of the war.[238] The efforts of the men and women who worked in the Office of the Provost Marshal General to set up and operate over 500 camps across the continental United States in only a few months is nothing short of a miracle.

An evaluation of the reeducation program at the end of the war spawned mixed opinions on how successful it actually was. One thought is the same among those who thought the program was a success. That as long as one prisoner had an effect on a German policy decision, then the program was a success.[239] But much of the proof of the success of the program was based on surveys that had no pre-program data to compare. The continuous shifting of the definition for the term "Nazi" did not help either. The short amount of time from the start of the reeducation program in 1944 to 1946 is not really long enough to radically change someone's worldview.

The labor program in comparison was very successful. German POWs worked on hundreds of farms across the country, saving millions of dollars' worth of crops for the war effort. The interaction with American civilians gave many POWs a chance to view the United States in person rather than in a classroom

---

238. Krammer, *Nazi Prisoners of War,* 256.
239. Gansburg, *Stalag: USA,* 180.

64

or fighting on the battlefield. The separation from the POW officers in the camps allowed the rank-and-file soldier to relax a bit more and interact with others. The general kindness shown to the POWs by American farmers across the United States did more to show the wealth and prosperity of the American way of life then the reeducation program could do in a classroom under the watchful eyes of the Nazi officers.

Overall the effects of the labor program on a German POW's view of the United States cannot be overstated. By allowing the POWs to see for themselves what America really looked like without the propaganda of Nazi Germany, the labor program allowed the POW to form his own conclusions on American Democracy. The reeducation program tried to use a position of authority to tell the POWs what American democracy was like. The labor program let him decide for himself in a manner that could not be faked. In the end it is better to show than tell.

APPENDIX

Appendix 1: "The Inner Power" by Julian Ritter

The crisis of our times has political and economic causes. But it has other backgrounds too. It is true that questions of frontier corrections, of economics and technique are today of predominant importance and they draw the attention of the masses like huge bill boards. But often they occupy too large a part of our thinking. Man after all is not guided exclusively by the political and economic developments. There are in him spiritual powers, too, and these are directed towards other form of reality. Important above all is the inner urge to find basic answers to certain questions of life in this strange world. These questions are of a philosophical nature. They search for laws which are determined by reason. Moreover, a strong religious feeling is found in many persons. To some this gives a Stronger sense of security in the midst of the general insecurity; in others it arouses the desire to give a higher meaning to an increasingly mechanized existence. Others are drawn to art, to pure beauty, towards the cultivation of taste and the simple yet aesthetic molding of their environment. All these powers create genuine desires in men and only when they are satisfied, does the rounded picture of a personality emerge.

Quite correctly we speak today of the "massification" of man. This mass-man is characterized by his incompleteness. Compared to a full statue he seems like a torso. His increased concern with politics has pushed aside two powers within him: his power of judgment and his depth of thought, and thus his life as member of a community is affected.

It is not always his own fault if this has happened. In a certain narrower sense the full development of his personality has been hindered by the difficulty of the times, by the one-sidedness of education and by the over-specialized division of labor. Yet his own weakness of character, his lack of decision, and his confusion too must be blamed. For man is by no means only and entirely the product of his environment, his inner life he owes to a creative initiative exclusively his own. There is in each human being something resembling a seismograph sensitive to disturbances of his inner being. He is discontent, even though his material necessities are satisfied. A nameless sense of discomfort tortures him. And when in hours of leisure he looks into his soul he often finds an emptiness which disquiets him still more. And in vain will he try to comfort himself by mere noise of words. The discomfort remains. And for the sake of escape, of distraction he then follows whichever voices cry hardest in his surroundings.

As soon, however, as a man becomes conscious of this situation he will begin to detach himself from the anonymous one-sidedness of mass being. Noisy slogans with which he was wont to drug his conscience no longer satisfy him. He not only becomes critical – he becomes critical of himself. His inner understanding of environment and society becomes deeper and freer.

With this first step towards the development of his power of judgment man as a personality is born anew. In order to form such an independent power of judgment one must try to accustom oneself to examine critically each fact and each opinion. A delicate balancing of ideas is thus the basis of all true judgment. But although skeptical examination and observation will tend to make a man's spirit free, yet these do not make it mature and sovereign. And if he stops with these he will merely make arbitrary judgments and will easily become arrogant.

In addition to all this one more thing is necessary: experience. Life will give this experience, but not a man's own life experience alone. The great thinkers of all time transmit to us their own experiences and with them those of many centuries, long gone. They give us an opportunity to study advantages and disadvantages and to sharpen our concepts. With their help we can free ourselves from the fatal tyranny of slogans. And critically we create our own picture of the world. We avoid half-truths which will often lead us astray in our personal lives. The truth of that is apparent from a glance at Goethe's maxims and reflections, Schiller's essay on the legislation of Lycurgus, the aphorisms of Schopenhauer and Lichtenberg, or Wilhelm Raabe's novels. Such reading leads to spiritual freedom. We must read without bias, in order to reach that freedom of the spirit which – in the words of Kant – is the strongest foundation of a personality. And yet it is necessary that still another power be developed within a man's soul – that of a mature thoughtfulness.

A soul guided only by appetite breeds dangerous passions – anger, envy, hatred. World history teaches that man has been truly creative only when he has cultivated the positive qualities of the soul such as kindness, understanding, integration, and conciliation. To accomplish this a self-discipline is needed which can be developed in daily intercourse with his neighbors if he accustoms himself to pay attention to such humble qualities as tact, true modesty, and tolerance towards the opinions of others.

One of the characteristics of our time is suspicion. Very easily and immediately one scents in other men the enemy. Defense against imagined enemies, often even against well-meaning friends is a permanent state of mind. Any other attitude appears dangerous because of one's own intolerance, and rudeness seems the easiest way to rid oneself of other peoples' opinions. Patient understanding and appreciation of another person's world, however, opens the soul. The melancholy will become more cheerful. Moodiness and self-pity yield to beneficent humor. And finally, nourished by wisdom and love, the spirit of enterprise grows – that spirit more vital for future constructive work than endless discussion and barren theory.

We know that it is the simple truths which have inspired our forefathers to truly noble deeds. It is theses which awaken those powers which will prove most trustworthy in the building of our future.[240]

---

240. Julian Ritter, "The Inner Powers," *Der Ruf,* no. 1 (March 1, 1945): 1, Records of the Provost Marshall General, Record Group 389, Box 1598; National Archives at College Park, College Park, MD. 1-2.

BIBLIOGRAPHY

Primary Sources

Records of the Provost Marshall General. Enemy POW Information Bureau, Executive Division, POW Special Projects Division, Prisoner of War Operations Div. Record Group 389. National Archives at College Park, College Park, MD.

Frankenmuth Historical Association. POW Letter Collection. Frankenmuth, MI.

Interview with Mike K. by Anita B., Prisoners of World War II," Frankenmuth Historical Association.

Lakeshore Museum Center. POW Letter Collection. Muskegon, MI.

Lynn Ahrens and Marv Herzog, Written statement by Verna Van Develde, February 1995. Frankenmuth Historical Association.

International Committee of the Red Cross. "Convention relative to the treatment of Prisoners of War." Geneva, 27 July 1929. Accessed November 2016. https://ihldatabases.icrc.org/applic/ihl/ihl.nsf/Treaty.xsp?action=open-Document&documentId=BDEDDD046FDEBA9C12563CD002D69B1

Proud, Philip, "A Study of the Reeducation of German Prisoners of War at Fort Custer, Michigan, 1945-1946," Master's Thesis, University of Michigan, 1949.

Newspapers

New York Times

Secondary Sources

A.B. Love and H.P. Gaston, "Michigan's Emergency Farm Labor, 1943-1947,"
    Extension Bulletin 288, (Michigan State College-Extension Service,
    December 1947).

Billinger, Robert. *Hitler's Soldiers in the Sunshine State.* Florida: University
    Press of Florida, 2000.

Breen, Lynne and Floeter, Ernst, *I'll See You Again, Lady Liberty.* California:
    WingSpan Press, 2014.

Carlson, Lewis. *We Were Each Other's Prisoners.* Basic Books, 1997.

Custodis, Johann. "Employing the enemy: the contribution of German and Italian
    Prisoners of War to British agriculture during and after the Second World
    War." *Agricultural History Review* 60, no. 2 (2012): 243-265. Accessed
    April 3, 2018: http://www.bahs.org.uk/AGHR/ARTICLES/60_2_8_cus-
    todis.pdf

Gansberg, Judith. *Stalag: U.S.A.* New York: Thomas Y. Crowell Company, 1977.
Hall, Kevin. "The Befriended Enemy: German Prisoners of War In Michigan."
    Michigan Historical Review 41, No. 1 (Spring 2015). http://www.jstor.
    org/stable/10.5342/michhistrevi.41.1.0057

Hahn, Lauran. "Germans in the Orchards: Post-World War II Letters from Ex-
    POW Agricultural Workers to a Midwestern Farmer." *The Journal of the
    Midwest Modern Language Association* 33/34, no. 3/4. (Autumn, 2000 –
    Winter, 2001). http://www.jstor.org/stable/1315350

Krammer, Arnold. *Nazi Prisoners of War in America.* Maryland: Scarborough
    House / Publishers, 1996.

Kruger, Cole. "Stalag Nebraska: Labor and Education Programs in Nebraska's
    World War II Prisoner of War Camps." Master Dissertation, University of
    Nebraska, 2014.

Lewis, George and Mewha, John. *History of Prisoner of War Utilization by the*

United States Army 1776-1945. Hawaii: University Press of the Pacific, 2002.

Lowe, William. "Working for Eighty Cents a Day: German Prisoners of War in Michigan, 1943-1946," Master thesis, Eastern Michigan University, 1995.

Murphy, Raymond E., Francis B. Stevens, Howard Trivers and Joseph M. Roland, *National Socialism: Basic Principles, Their Application By The Nazi Party's Foreign Organization, And The Use Of Germans Abroad For Nazi Aims* (Washington, United States Government Printing Office, 1943).

Murphy, Karen. "Teaching as Persuasion: A New Metaphor for a New Decade," *Theory Into Practice* 40, No. 4. (Autumn, 2001): 224-227. Accessed January 21, 2018, http://www.jstor.org/stable/1477483.

Pepin, John. "POW Camps in the U.P." *Marquette Mining Journal* (2000). Accessed March 3, 2017: http://wnmutv.nmu.edu/media/pow_book72.pdf

Robin, Ron. *The Barbed-Wire College*. New Jersey: Princeton University Press, 1995.

Smith, Arthur. *The War for the German Mind: Re-educating Hitler's Soldiers,* Oxford: Berghahn Books, 1996.

Swallow, Greg. "Camp Raco: A case study of power and domination in the Upper Peninsula of Michigan / Greg Swallow," Master Thesis, Central Michigan University, 2018.

War Department, *Facts Vs Fantasy* (Washington: United States Government Printing Office, 1944).

Yelich Biniecki, Susan M. and Simone C. O. Conceicao, "How living or traveling to foreign locations influences adults' worldviews and impacts personal identity," *New Horizons In Adult Education & Human Resource Development* 26, no. 3 (2014): 39-53, accessed January 20, 2018, http://web.a.ebscohost.com.cmich.idm.oclc.org/ehost/detail/detail?vid=0&sid=67fbdbd0-eb26-44ee-ab88-789a5b00d6e1%40sessionmgr4010&bdata=-JnNpdGU9ZWhvc3QtbGl2ZQ%3d%3d#AN=97162841&db=ofs

Znamenski, Andrei. ""National Socialists" to "Nazi": History, Politics, and the English Language," *The Independent Review* 19, No. 4 (Spring 2015): 537-561, accessed January 20, 2018, http://www.jstor.org/stable/24563068